Anthony Huberman

[AH.2015]

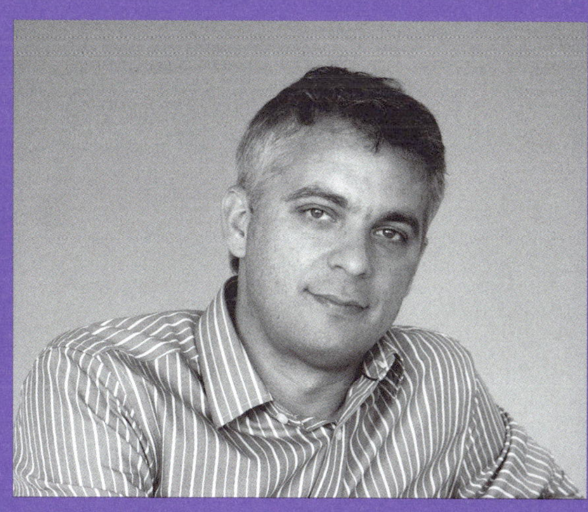

Courtesy Anthony Huberman

PAGE 11

TYPE Essay

TITLE *PAY ATTENTION MOTHERFUCKERS* (2015)

AAM HISTORY Formerly Director of the Artist's Institute, New York, Anthony Huberman is now Director and Chief Curator of the CCA Wattis Institute, San Francisco. Huberman's contribution here expands on a previously published essay in *frieze*. His appearance in our initial issue of *Permanent Collection* marks his first direct connection with the museum.

Marcel Broodthaers

[MB.2014]

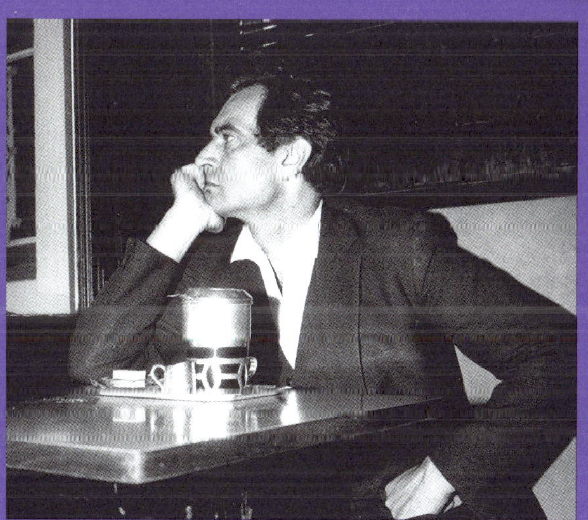

Courtesy the Estate of Marcel Broodthaers

PAGE 23

TYPE Interview

TITLE *Interview with Marcel Broodthaers by Marcel Broodthaers* (1970)

AAM HISTORY Marcel Broodthaers (1924–1976) was a Belgian artist and poet who declared himself the director of his own imagined institution, the Musée de l'Art Moderne, Départment des Aigles. The Aspen Art Museum presented Broodthaers's exhibition *Décor: A Conquest* from December 20, 2014–March 8, 2015, originally conceived in 1974 as the inaugural show for the ICA, London.

Simon Denny [SD.2012]

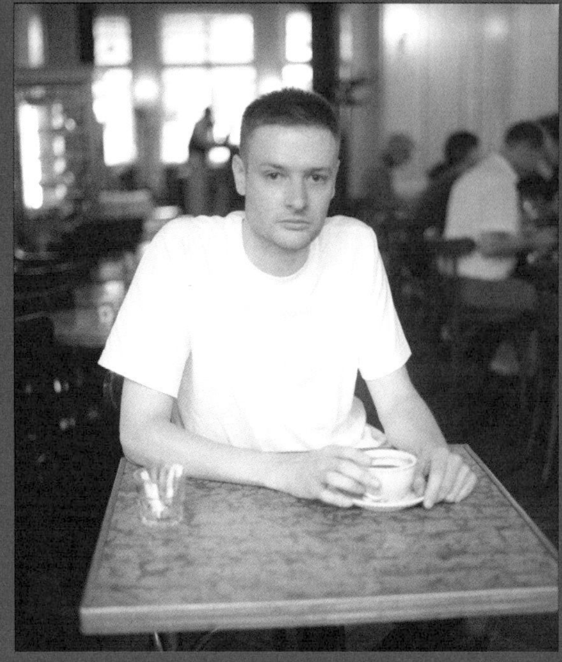

Photo: Calla Henkel and Max Pitegoff

PAGE 29

TYPE Visual Essay

TITLE *Secret Power: Unpacking Original Visual Content in the Snowden NSA Slides* (2016)

AAM HISTORY Artist Simon Denny was born in Auckland, New Zealand, in 1982, and currently lives and works in Berlin, Germany. Denny's Aspen Art Museum exhibition, *Full Participation*, was on view from May 18–July 15, 2012. His AAM show grew, in part, out of his research into the history of Aspen's own GrassRoots Television, the oldest community-access cable channel in the country. One video featured GrassRoots footage of Aspen luminary Nick DeWolf speaking about the electronic community bulletin board system that he designed and implemented at the station in 1980–81.

Laura Hoptman [LH.2008]

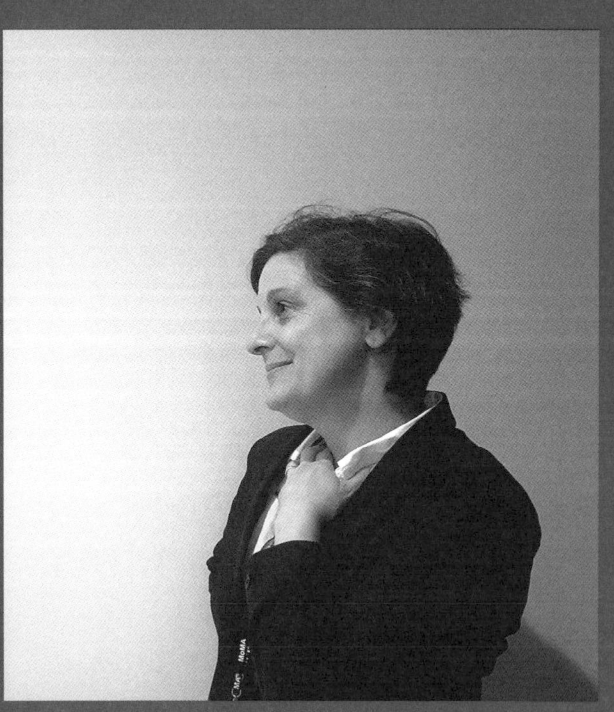

Photo: Kelsey Knutson

PAGE 50

TYPE Essay

TITLE *Contentious Curating: Contemporary Painting at MOMA* (2015)

AAM HISTORY Laura Hoptman is the Department of Painting and Sculpture Curator at the Museum of Modern Art. Hoptman's first interaction with the Aspen Art Museum was in 2008. Hoptman, along with guest curators Dan Cameron and Lauri Firstenberg, juried the exhibition *ARAC@ AAM: Anderson Ranch at the Aspen Art Museum*, a group show that was on view from October 31– December 7, 2008.

Betty Woodman   [BW.1984]

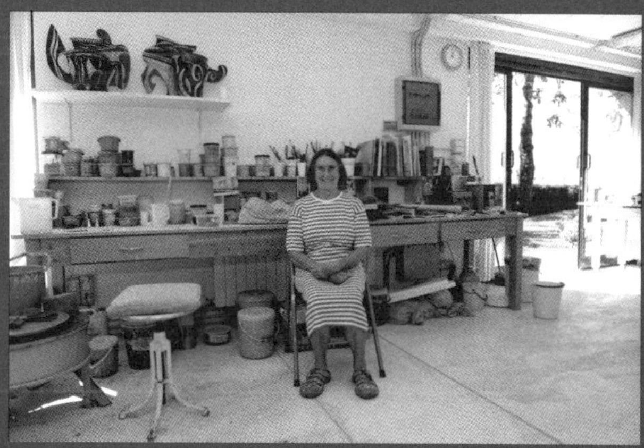
Photo: Stefano Porcinai

PAGE 58

TYPE Interview

TITLE *Betty Woodman in conversation with Heidi Zuckerman* (2016)

AAM HISTORY Artist Betty Woodman was born in 1930, in Connecticut, and currently lives and works in New York. Woodman's Aspen Art Museum show, *The Aspen Garden Room*, was on view from March 24–June 24, 1984. Presented in the former AAM's galleries (located in the historical Holy Cross Power Plant), the exhibition was one of Woodman's first to examine the illusion of space with objects such as columns and frames—an aspect of the artist's practice that continues today.

Rodney Graham   [RG.2016]

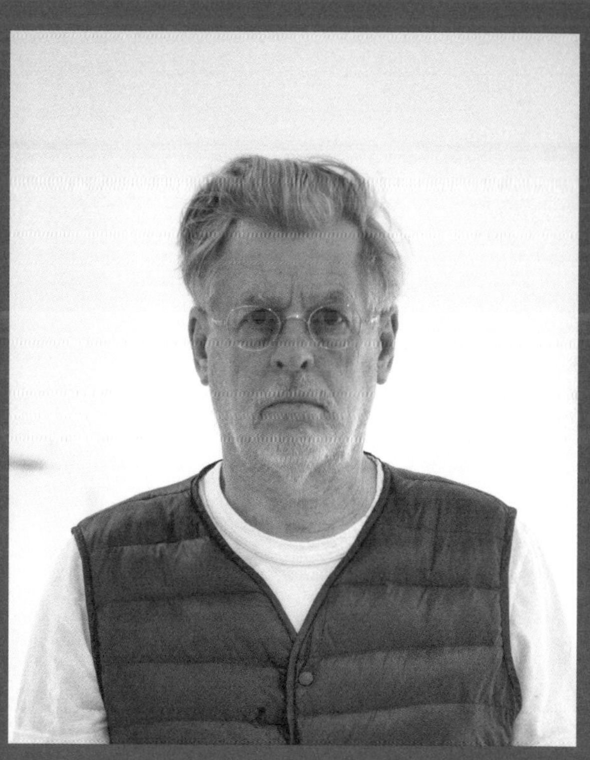
Photo: Scott Livingston

PAGE 64

TYPE Essay

TITLE *Fig. 0* (2016)

AAM HISTORY Canadian artist Rodney Graham, born in 1949, lives and works in Vancouver. A version of Graham's essay, included here, was given as a short talk during a panel discussion on Broodthaers, May 4, 2016, at the Museum of Modern Art, New York. This edition of *Permanent Collection* marks Graham's first instance of working with the Aspen Art Museum.

Sarah Rifky [SR.2014]

PAGE 76

TYPE Lecture (Essay)

TITLE *Keywords to Talking* (2015)

AAM HISTORY Sarah Rifky is an Egypt-based writer and curator who was Codirector of *Beirut*, an initiative and exhibition space in Cairo that closed in 2015. In 2014, Rifky led a discussion at the Aspen Art Museum centered on institution-building as a curatorial act as well as on political, economic, educational, and ecological issues surrounding the arts. Her piece *Keywords to Talking*, included in this issue of *Permanent Collection*, comes from a text that was originally drafted for the 2014 discussion.

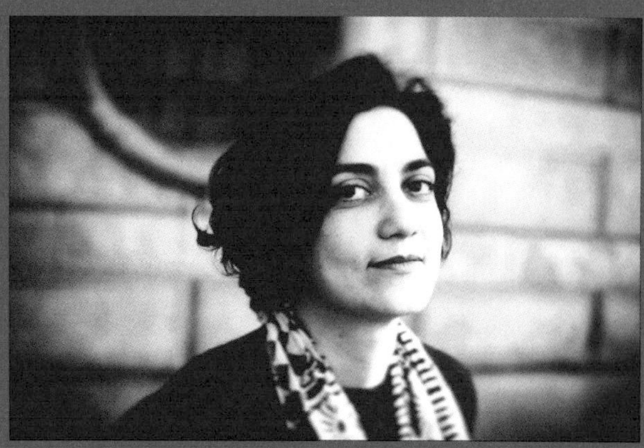

Photo: Jacob Crawfurd

Director's Foreword

For many, the museum and the collection naturally go hand-in-hand. If there is a concept that remains more elusive within visual arts institutional practice, it is that of the non-collecting museum. The Aspen Art Museum (AAM) was founded thirty-seven years ago as a non-collecting institution modeled on the European *kunsthalle* ("art hall"). Rooted within Aspen and focused on presenting important contemporary art from around the world, the AAM is an incubator of ideas, serving as a platform for a broad variety of voices. It is an institution focused on fostering dialogue that upends the expected and celebrates the contradictory.

Taking our distinct institutional structure into account, we decided to bring together a publication series that hones in on the ideas that we collect. Published twice a year, *Permanent Collection* draws from the museum's programming, but does so in discursive ways by digging deeper into specific subjects. Past, present, and future intersect through both newly commissioned and previously published essays, texts, interviews, transcriptions, images, ephemera, asides, and more.

Our first issue fittingly turns attention to the concept of "institutionality." The texts here address the diverse possibilities of institutional practice, as seen through the eyes of artists, curators, and writers—ranging from the analytically objective to the poetically and singularly subjective. The complexities of how we look at art objects within the context of institutions are explored here—how we "frame" them, under what conditions, and how various circumstances (historical, geographical, critical, cultural, or even political) affect our experiences of them.

We begin with an interview in which the late founder of New York's New Museum, Marcia Tucker, and I discuss the work of contemporary artist Richard Tuttle, as well as the larger issues of visual literacy and the transformative power of art itself. This is followed by CCA Wattis Director Anthony Huberman's revised version of his confrontationally titled essay *PAY ATTENTION MOTHERFUCKERS*. Both explore what happens in the presence of art or when we experience artworks that shake us loose from notions we assumed were fixed or finite.

Sarah Rifky, cofounder of the now closed Cairo-based art space *Beirut*, expands on her talk at the AAM in 2014, considering the ways in which institutions and artists can, could, or should be revolutionary agents. Rifky points out that the root of the word "institution" comes from the Latin word meaning "to establish" or "cause to stand," and art itself is not only an "aggregator," but also a known and welcome "aggravator."

Curator Laura Hoptman was given the opportunity to revisit her recent group exhibition of contemporary abstract paintings at MoMA, *The Forever

Now: Contemporary Painting in an Atemporal World, which generated some heated critiques. She deftly sifts through the possible subtexts and origins of the critiques themselves, and examines how critical prejudices might shape perspectives of an exhibition of "suspect" objects.

There are also the voices of artists, beginning with a reprint of Marcel Broodthaers's rigorous, but playful 1970 interview of himself. An inventive self-interrogation, the dialogue is supplemented by artist Rodney Graham's equally poetic rumination on the surreal path Broodthaers's work often took to find its way into the world. Simon Denny, who examined broader concepts of institutionality, created a visual essay on the archival illustrations accompanying the 2013 "leaked" US National Security Administration documents by political dissident Edward Snowden. Finally, Betty Woodman recently restaged a variation of her 1984 AAM exhibition, *The Aspen Garden Room*—a multimedia installation encompassing elements of her ceramic works—and our conversation examines how expansive both artistic practice and exhibition can become.

I thank all those that have contributed their time, words, and energy to launch *Permanent Collection* and their assistance in what will ultimately be an illuminating and thought-provoking new initiative. I always advocate that the AAM remain a place for slowing down and even stopping, to reflect and to question. While reading *Permanent Collection*, I urge the same thing I would within our Aspen galleries: take your time—time to allow the visible and the invisible, the tangible and the ephemeral to converge. Time enough to realize Anthony Huberman's notion that doing so may, ultimately, lead you to a place where "clarifications and contradictions both have time to accumulate, and neither cancels one another out." A place where a non-collecting museum may also have a *Permanent Collection*.

See you at the Aspen Art Museum.

—Heidi Zuckerman
Nancy and Bob Magoon CEO and Director

Marcia Tucker

in conversation with Heidi Zuckerman

In 1975, the final (and most personally consequential) exhibition that Marcia Tucker would curate at the Whitney Museum of American Art focused on the work of Richard Tuttle, an artist whose practice had yet to be fully accepted in the US. The interview that follows between Heidi Zuckerman and Tucker took place in Aspen in January 2006, and focuses on the work of Tuttle, who had an exhibition in the Lower Gallery of the AAM at the time.

Heidi Zuckerman The San Francisco Museum of Modern Art has organized a major retrospective of Richard Tuttle's work, currently on view at the Whitney and traveling to a number of other prominent museums across the country. For such a long time, Richard's work was seen as being outside the mainstream parameters of contemporary art. Can you talk about where you first saw his work and what decisions you made to do that initial show at the Whitney in 1975?

Marcia Tucker I think I first saw it at Betty Parsons Gallery, which was, in certain ways, conventional, and then in other ways, surprisingly unconventional. I have to admit that I'm always drawn to what I don't understand. If there's real resistance on my part, then I'm intrigued enough to go back and really find out why there is resistance.

With Richard's work, I didn't understand anything I was looking at. It had no relationship to what was touted as important, major art at that time. It was made of very modest and unprepossessing materials and wasn't representational. It didn't look like anything I'd seen before, except it had a curious kind of resonance in the real world— almost resembling bits of garbage, but not quite. Over the years, I was really moved to follow the work and establish a relationship with Richard, and finally, of course, to do a show, which was my intention in the first place.

I have to say something about exhibitions. There are two ways of doing them: you can make an exhibition didactically, i.e., you learn about something and then present and share what you know; or you can do it investigatively, which means that through the organization of that exhibition, you hope to find out more, so the exhibition in itself is a learning process. With Richard's work, it seemed that the latter was the proper way.

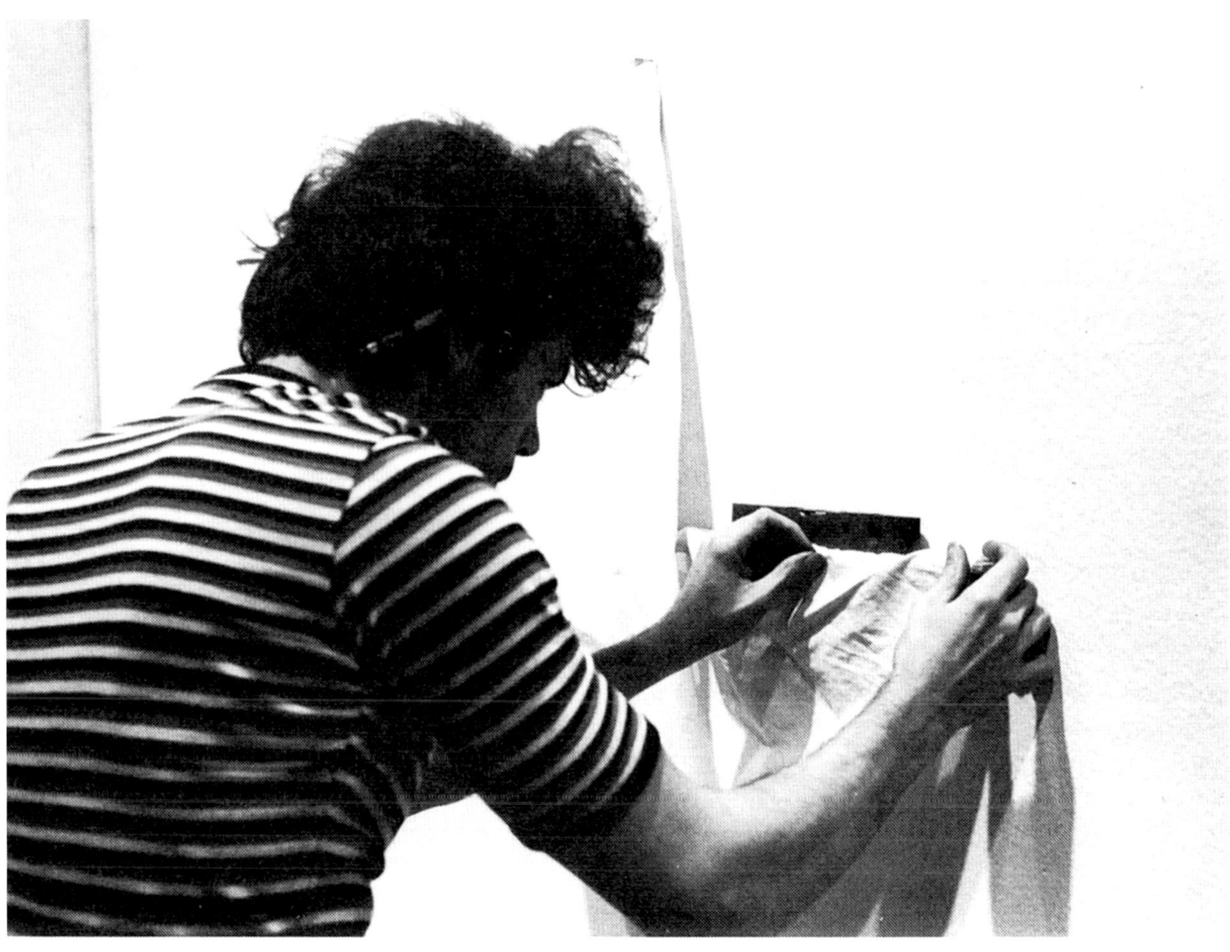

HZ Richard really likes to collaborate with curators. What was that like during the first show?

MT To work with Richard—and with many of the artists whose work I've really loved and who I've spent a lot of time with—was, in the deepest sense, a collaboration. I also do not have any illusions about being an artist myself; I'm a facilitator as a curator. In some ways, I'm an entrepreneur trying to help make an exhibition happen. I would say that it's a kind of friendship that doesn't exist in my other friendships, no matter how deep.

When I was a child, I had a fantasy (really, it's a lifelong fantasy) of going through somebody's head and fitting my body to theirs and looking out through their eyes, but at the same time through my own. That's what that friendship or collaboration is like. I am the curator who is trying to help make this exhibition happen in a way that makes sense, but I also begin to see the world again through the artist's eyes. That's what it was like with Richard. It

Richard Tuttle installing *4th Summer Wood Piece*, 1974. Second installation (October 7–November 3, 1975) of *Richard Tuttle* (September 12–November 16, 1975). Whitney Museum of American Art, New York. Photo: Geoffrey Clements

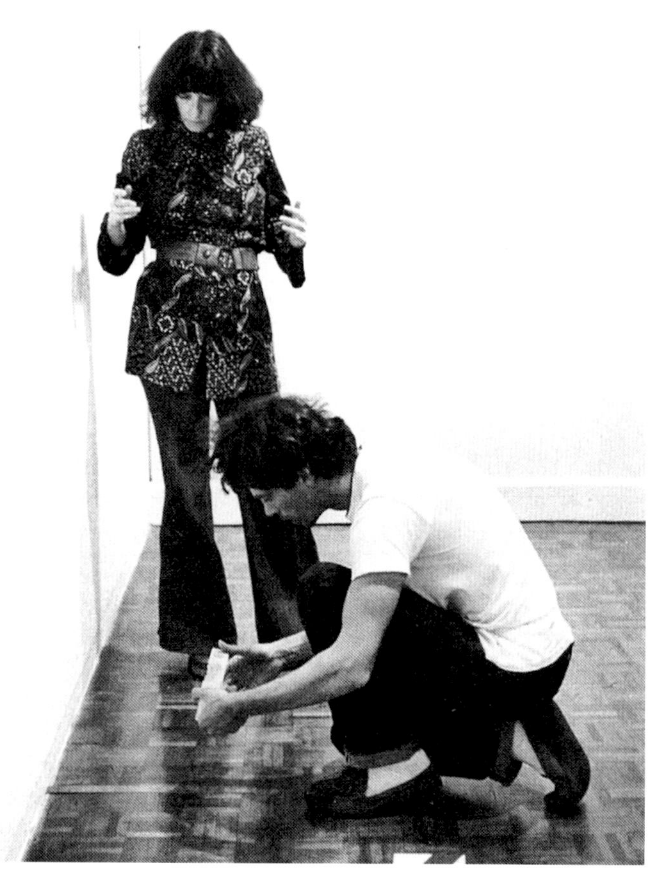

was also fun. He is a wonderful person who you want to spend time around. I've been around very difficult artists and learned to love them and to adjust, but Richard is nothing but a joy and pleasure to work with. I'm sure that you've found that, too.

HZ Yes. I've learned so many things from Richard in the time that I've had the great honor of working with him, which isn't that long. He's really a true artist in the sense that he has a vision that is art and also so much more than art. It's about the world and the importance of everything that is visible and invisible, about trying to make the world a better place, about taking a stand, but not in a didactic way. He's a real advocate for the power of art and for its ability to effect change in a positive way in the world.

Marcia Tucker, curator of exhibition, with Richard Tuttle, installing *Block Pieces* (1973) for the third installation (November 4–16, 1975) of *Richard Tuttle* (September 12–November 16, 1975). Whitney Museum of American Art, New York. Photo: Geoffrey Clements

[MT.1967] [HZ.2005]

MT   When the critics—who were very harsh about Richard's first Whitney exhibition—said things like, "Tuttle's work makes you scrutinize the teeny-weeny hairline cracks on the wall," I would think, "Right! Isn't that what it's all about?" It's like going to a great movie and when you come out, the world has changed and you see things very differently. That's what Richard's work made you do. What was a criticism, of course, turned out to be the very thing that the work was about.

I also think that Richard's interest in the quotidian, in the relationship of art to everyday experience, to real experience, is very important, and was quite different to dominating work at the time. It was an era of huge painting, monumental sculpture, and powerful things. His work was so unassuming and, in many cases, almost invisible. It forced people to come right up flat against their expectations and made many angry for that reason.

HZ   The quotidian is an element that's also apparent in some of the works in his AAM exhibition, using things that you would find every day. One of the points that he emphasizes is that art doesn't need to be precious; it doesn't need to be made out of things that are art like—things that you find in your everyday life can be elevated to the status of art.

MT   He also has this near-magical ability when you look at his work to make you think, "Oh! *I* could do that," instead of, "My child could do that." It develops a desire to make something. That modesty or humility and the sense of familiarity for the viewer is so reassuring. It takes art out of the realm of being something so high, out of reach, and precious that it doesn't have anything to do with the rest of us in the real world.

HZ   That point of relevance is really interesting. The idea that, through visual literacy and object-oriented learning, we can get people to look at the world in a different way essentially defines a successful exhibition as being one where visitors leave and see something they hadn't previously acknowledged. For example, at the new de Young Museum in San Francisco, one of the site-specific installations is a crack from the street all the way through the building—a crack actually can be art.

MT   If you can change the way you see—and you assume, as I do, that the eye, the heart, the mind, and the hand are either connected or the same thing—then you change who you are. That seems very powerful to me and that, in a way, is why art is so important.

HZ   Right. Our society, in many ways, is filled with people seeking to achieve personal transformation. Everyone's reading self-help books and trying to make themselves better—a noble quest indeed. But if we can succeed in putting art in unexpected places, then people may start to realize that, in art, there's this incredible power for transformation.

MT The other thing, of course, is that you don't have to know anything special. You can simply go and see or feel the ways in which your experience can be brought to bear on the experience of that work. It's not that difficult, it's only about a willingness to at least engage.

HZ Exactly, all people need is an open mind about what they see. That takes us right back to the title of our show, Art Matters—and it does.

[MT.1967] [HZ.2005]

Second installation (October 7–November 3, 1975) of *Richard Tuttle* (September 12–November 16, 1975). Whitney Museum of American Art, New York. Photo: Geoffrey Clements

Third installation (November 4–16, 1975) of *Richard Tuttle* (September 12–November 16, 1975). Whitney Museum of American Art, New York. Photo: Geoffrey Clements

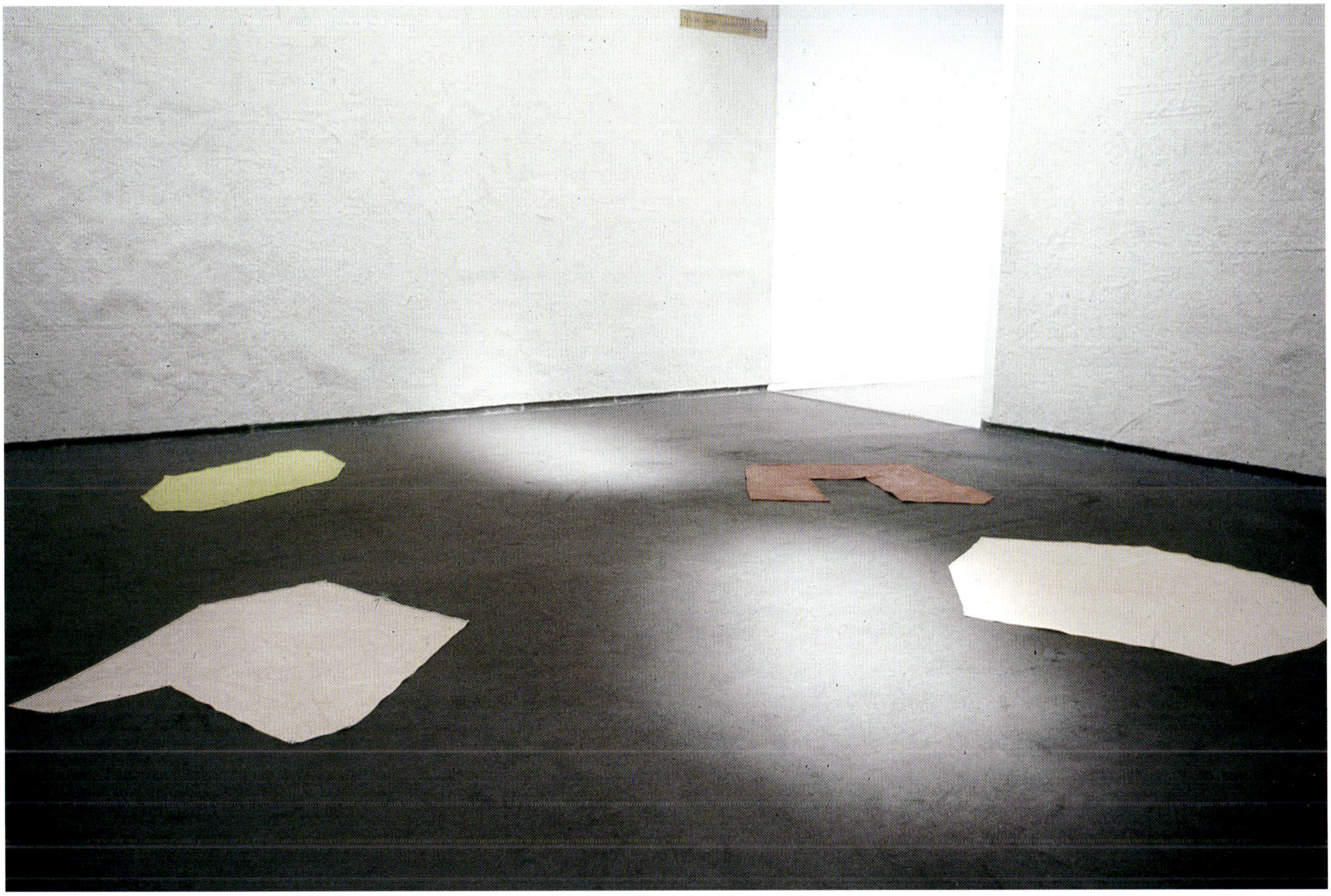

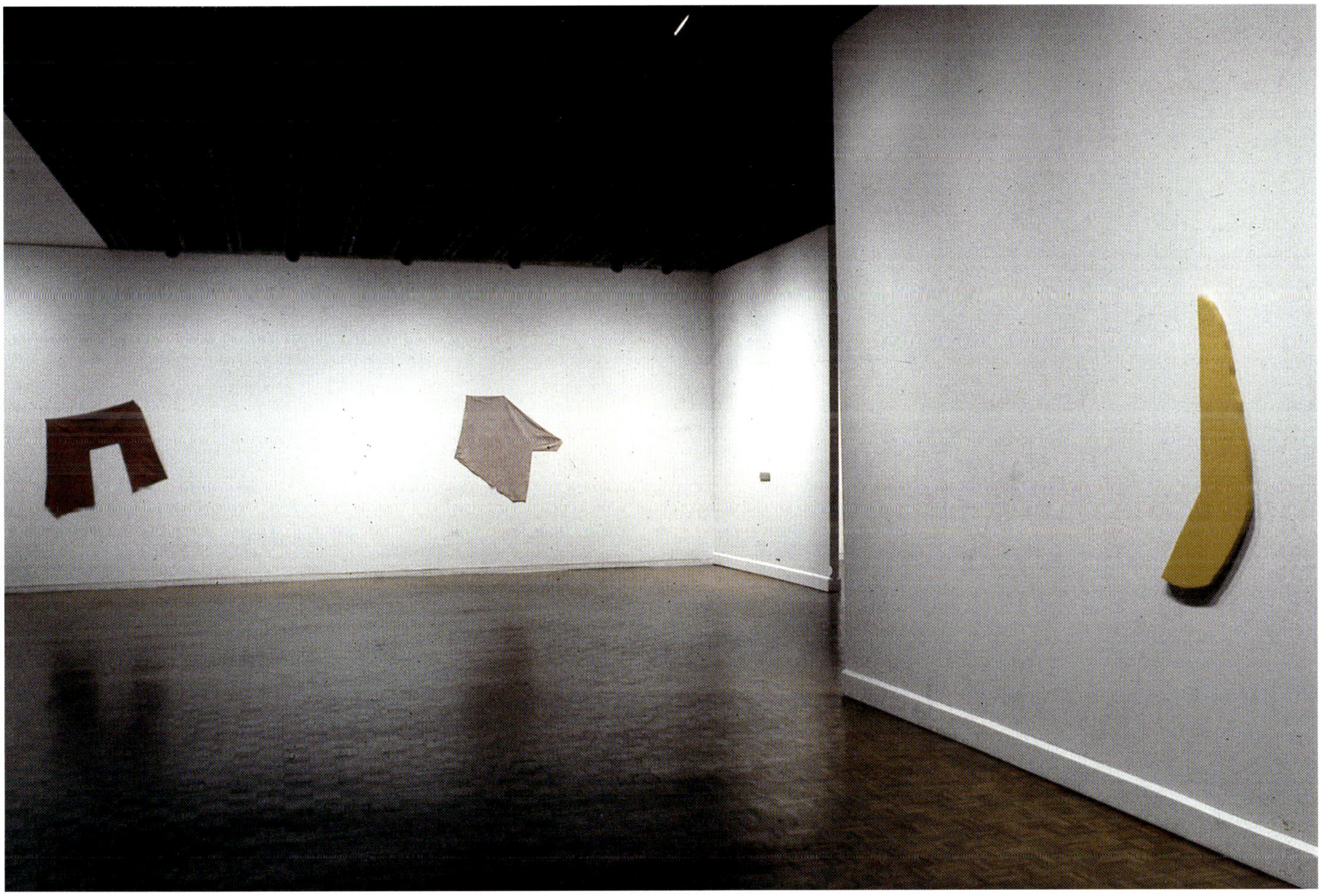

PAY
ATTENTION
MOTHER
FUCKERS

Anthony
Huberman

PAY ATTENTION MOTHERFUCKERS

A few years ago, the artist Matteo Callegari told me about Andy Kaufman's performance on *Saturday Night Live* on March 11, 1978. After informing the audience that he had been given the remaining twenty minutes of the live TV show to do whatever he wanted, Kaufman began reading F. Scott Fitzgerald's novel *The Great Gatsby*. "Chapter one," he began, and cleared his throat. "In my younger and more vulnerable years, my father gave me some advice that I've been turning over in my mind ever since," he continued, and kept reading until the audience became restless and started to heckle him. After a few minutes and a few more interruptions, Lorne Michaels, the show's producer, walked up and told Kaufman to stop. Before leaving the stage, the comedian proposed playing a record instead, eliciting cheers from the audience. Once the record began, they heard Kaufman's voice reading *The Great Gatsby*, beginning right from where he had left off. Everyone laughed—fade to commercial.

The reason this is funny, of course, is because it doesn't cohere with the way culture often gets consumed—people prefer the short-and-sweet over the long-and-dry, especially when it comes to their TV comedy shows. Yet, Kaufman's performance hints at how disruptive it would actually be for someone to intervene within a medium usually dedicated to quick consumption and ask an audience to pay attention to a single thing for an extended period of time.

The art historian Jeremiah McCarthy once made a related proposition to me when he suggested placing fifteen chairs in front of a single photograph by Rosemarie Trockel and inviting people to simply come sit and look at it. A conversation might or might not happen, but nothing was to be predetermined—it was about spending time with a single work of art and paying close attention to it.

But "pay attention" is far too vague of a phrase. In what contemporary economists call our "attention economy," it applies to almost everything we do. We pay attention to fashion trends, stock market fluctuations, or the sound of a child's cough; while, at the very same time, the local chain store wants us to pay attention to its lowered prices, the car dashboard wants us to pay attention to its engine light, and Twitter wants us to pay attention to something different every few seconds.

Bruce Nauman, *Pay Attention*, 1973. Lithograph, 38 1/4 x 28 1/4 in (97.2 x 71.8 cm). © 2016 Bruce Nauman / Artists Right Society (ARS). Courtesy Sperone Westwater, New York

The Kaufman and Trockel examples, on the other hand, strip attention down to its basic unit: a single book or a single photograph—and nothing else. This holds its charge in the fact that there are many other possible books or photographs with which to spend one's time, not to mention any number of other activities, objects, or people, but all of those options have been removed. In Tony Conrad's music or Michael Snow's films, for example, a single note or a single shot can make up the entire piece, and it's the extreme nature of the commitment to a specific choice that gives the work its power—on a conceptual, visual, experiential, and physical level. We all usually find ourselves surrounded by options, and so we quickly notice the moments when all of them have been taken away.

Artists use a range of methods to concentrate attention on a single chosen subject. The examples mentioned so far make use of duration—the artistic incarnation of the political filibuster—where audiences can only watch and wait. In addition to works by Conrad or Snow, one could point to James Benning's single-shot ninety-eight-minute *Nightfall* (2012) that begins as the sun is going down and ends in near blackness; or to Sharon Lockhart's *Double Tide* (2009), where a single clam digger searches the mudflats, or her *Lunchbreak* (2008), with its slowed-down single shot of a narrow hallway in a ship-building plant.

Another method is repetition. In 1963, Andy Warhol got us to think about Elvis Presley—and therefore about celebrity culture, mass media, pop culture, America—simply by filling the Ferus Gallery in Los Angeles with nothing but dozens of Elvis's. Daniel Buren's stripes appear and reappear over and over again, generating a sameness that allows us to recognize the changing contingencies of their physical sites. And Thomas Bayrle wallpapers entire museum galleries with millions of identical images to form a disorienting pattern.

A third method would be distance, in the sense of physically placing an audience in a location that is far away from anything else. For her *Nova Scotia Beach Dance* performance (1971), Joan Jonas placed her audience on top of a cliff in rural Canada. And the only way to see Walter de Maria's *The Lightning Field* (1977), Nancy Holt's *Sun Tunnels* (1976), Robert Smithson's *Spiral Jetty* (1970), or Richard Serra's more recent *East-West/West-East* (2015) is to venture deep into vast and empty landscapes.

Perhaps the most obvious strategy is isolation. Many artists install a single object or image in a gallery, isolating it from anything else—an experience of focused attention that is made all the more dramatic when the object is small and the space is large. Sparse installations of sculptures and/or photographs by Danh Võ, Michael E. Smith, Trisha Donnelly, or Aaron Flint Jamison come to mind.

Yet another, however paradoxical, is setting up obstacles. The silk curtains that covered David Hammons's *Kool-Aid* drawings (2003), when

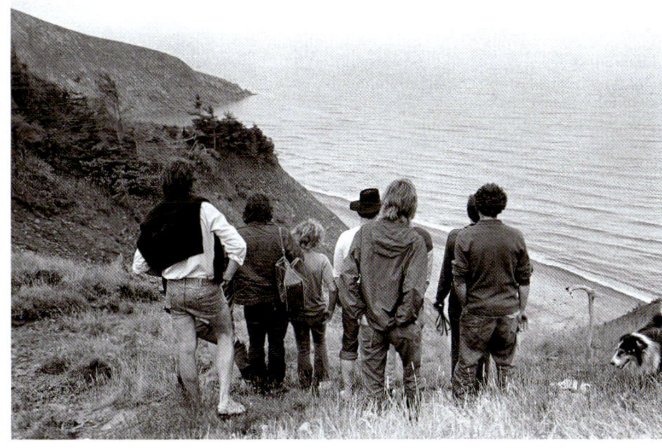
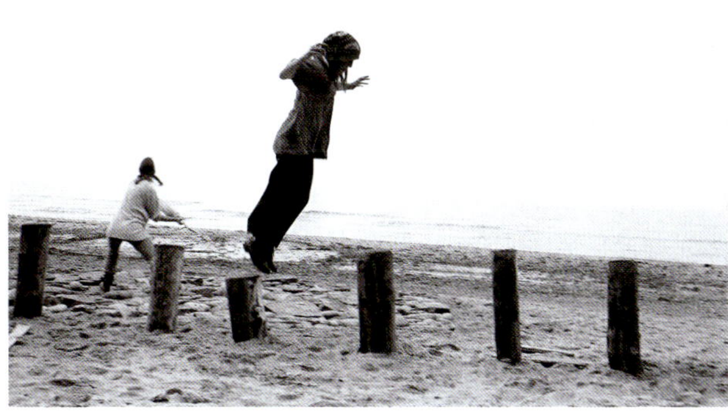
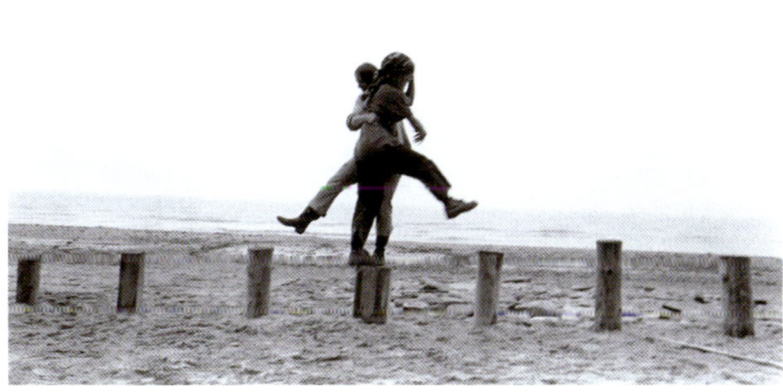
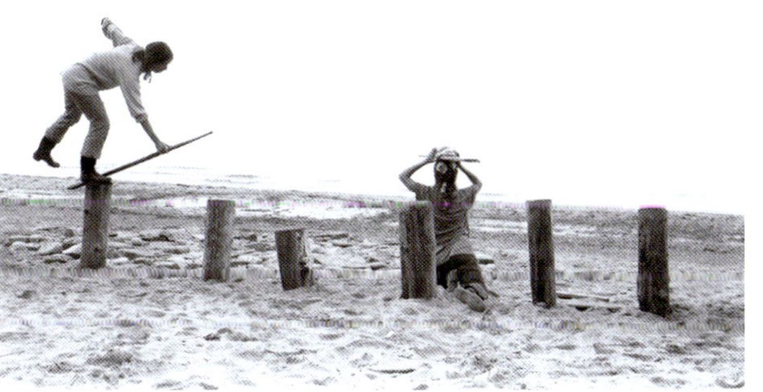

shown at the Museum of Modern Art in New York, could only be lifted by visitors who made an appointment and entered through a different entrance; or, more famously, Marcel Duchamp's *Étant donnés* (1946–66) lies hidden behind an old wooden door with only a small hole to glimpse through. These rituals guarantee an especially attentive viewing experience, once one makes it through everything that stands in the way of the work.

If artists value limiting choices and removing options, what would it mean for arts institutions to do the same? Traditionally, museums and galleries prefer the opposite—competing for funding, artists, press, and audience, many look to be as visible, diverse, popular, large, and active as possible. New York's MoMA PS1, for example, often has a dozen different exhibitions on view at any given time, while the ICA London's *fig-2* series involves a new exhibition every single week for fifty weeks. The Whitney Museum of American Art, the New Museum, MoMA, and the Metropolitan Museum of Art are all currently expanding their activities into new buildings.

Clearly, each of these institutions is offering invaluable opportunities to countless artists who deserve it. But what would it mean for an art center to say that visibility, scale, or productivity do not count among

Joan Jonas, *Nova Scotia Beach Dance*, 1971. Performance documentation by Richard Serra. Courtesy the artist and Wilkinson Gallery, London

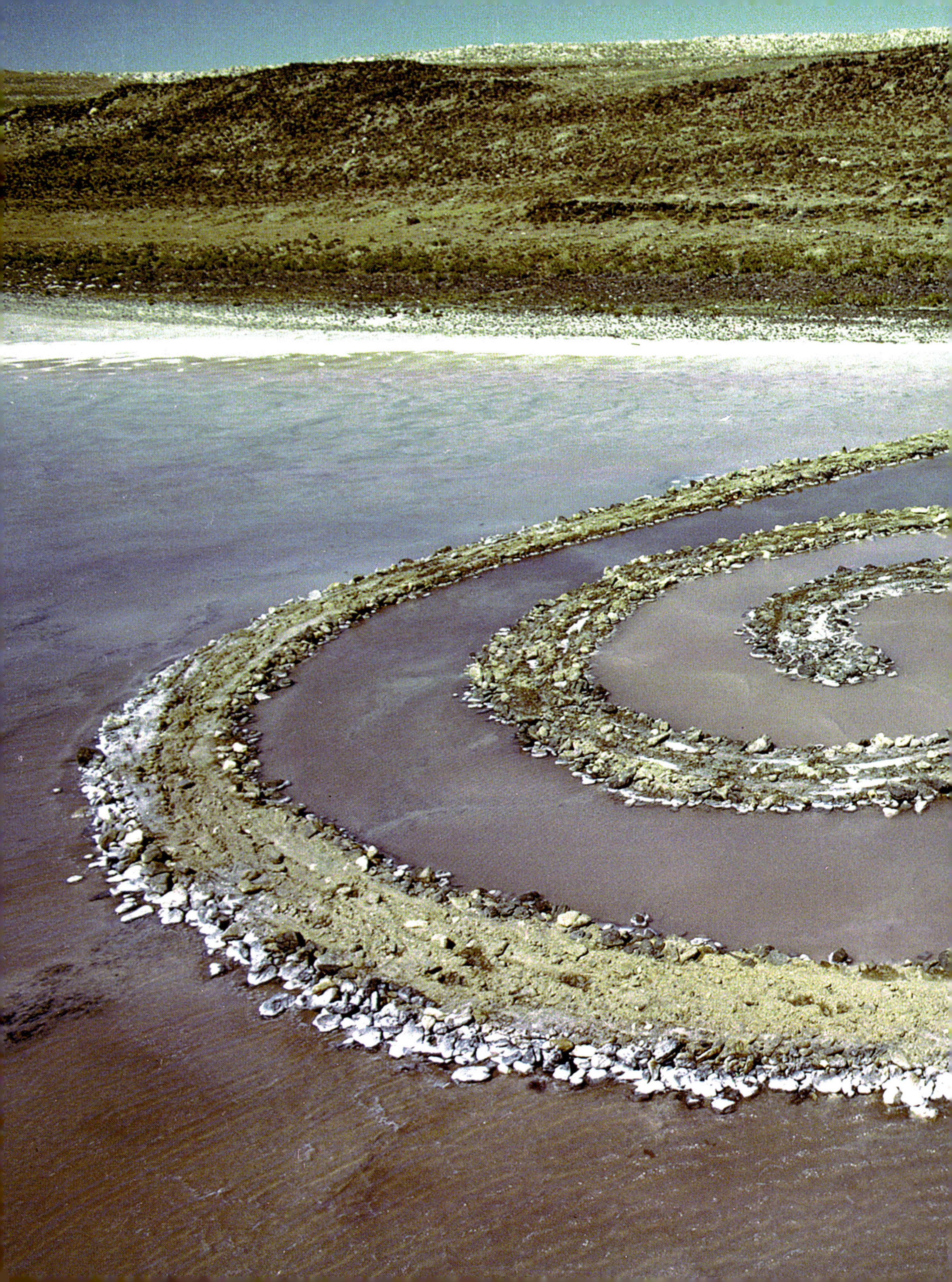

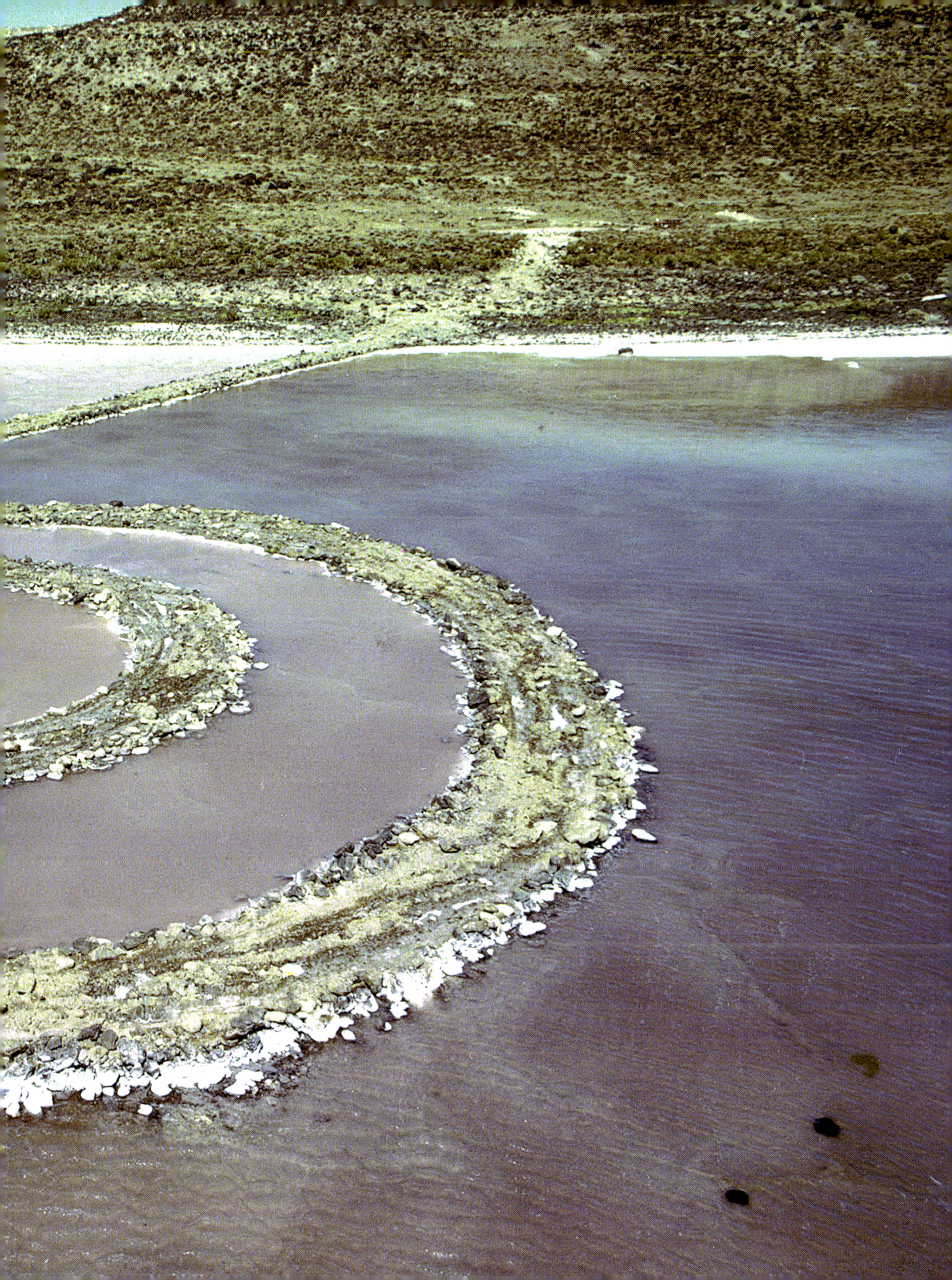

their criteria for success? Could a different politic of attention generate new types of art spaces? In examining these alternative institutional approaches—in spaces I would call "institutes"—a different set of priorities, or a certain code of conduct, begins to emerge: slowing down, staying small, repeating, making long-term commitments, and placing artists before all else. In what many might consider a perversion of commonly held values, a new breed of institution today appears to be scaling back in all senses of the term: in audience, in activity, in visibility, in online presence, in physical size—all in hopes of generating a scaling-up of rigor and focus, and what Kodwo Eshun calls "forms of attention." Instead of producing more content for more customers, they expect and demand more from their audience.

In 2010, with the support of Hunter College in New York, I founded a small art space and research institute, the Artist's Institute, where the Kaufman clip was shown and where people sat and looked at the Trockel. I hoped it could become an intimate place where people could step off the endless conveyer belt of the city's art exhibitions and spend time thinking about a single artist, even a single artwork, for an extended period of time. The concept was simple: each year would be divided into two six-month seasons, with each dedicated to a single artist. One work by that artist would be on view at a time, and it would change once per month. The goal was for this to be generative, and for the exhibited artist's work to open up discussions of other artists, writers, musicians, thinkers, and subjects.

The space I found for it was ideal: it was too small to be an exhibition gallery, and while it was street-level on the well-trafficked Lower East Side, its façade looked almost private, and would probably attract only those few who were actively looking for it. In other words, I could offer an artist a tiny quasi-basement space and very little money, but also a committed group of people who were going to spend six months paying close attention to their work.

The Artist's Institute has hosted seasons with Robert Filliou, Jo Baer, Jimmie Durham, Rosemarie Trockel, Haim Steinbach, Thomas Bayrle, and, under the leadership of Jenny Jaskey, with Lucy McKenzie, Pierre Huyghe, Carolee Schneemann, and Fia Backström. Despite the scale of the venue and budget, each of these well-known artists has accepted the invitation without hesitation—perhaps because it's precisely not an exhibition project, but something other and still undefined; perhaps because I was

PREVIOUS: Robert Smithson, *Spiral Jetty*, 1970. Great Salt Lake, Utah. Mud, salt crystals, rocks, water, 1500 x 15 ft (457.2 x 4.57 m). Photo: Gianfranco Gorgoni. Collection: DIA Center for the Arts, New York. Courtesy James Cohan Gallery, New York and Shanghai

David Hammons, *Kool-Aid Drawing*, 2004. Kool-Aid and pencil on paper, curtain, 43 x 28 3/4 in (109 x 73 cm). © David Hammons. Courtesy James Cohan Gallery, New York. Photo: Jason Mandella

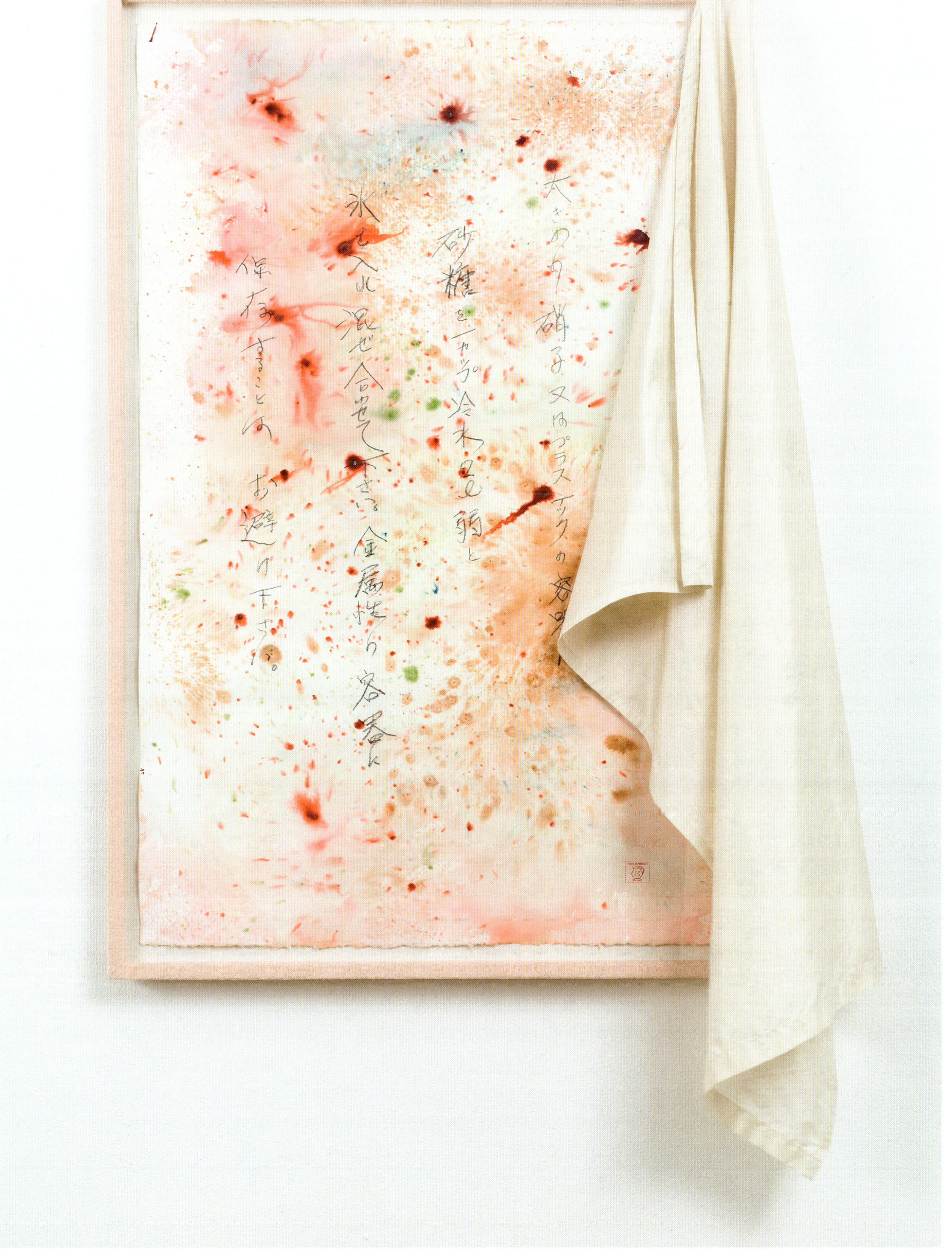

大きめの硝子又はプラスチックの容器に
砂糖を一カップ冷水豆玉弱と
氷を入れ混ぜ合せて下さい。金属性の容器に
保存することのお避け下さい。

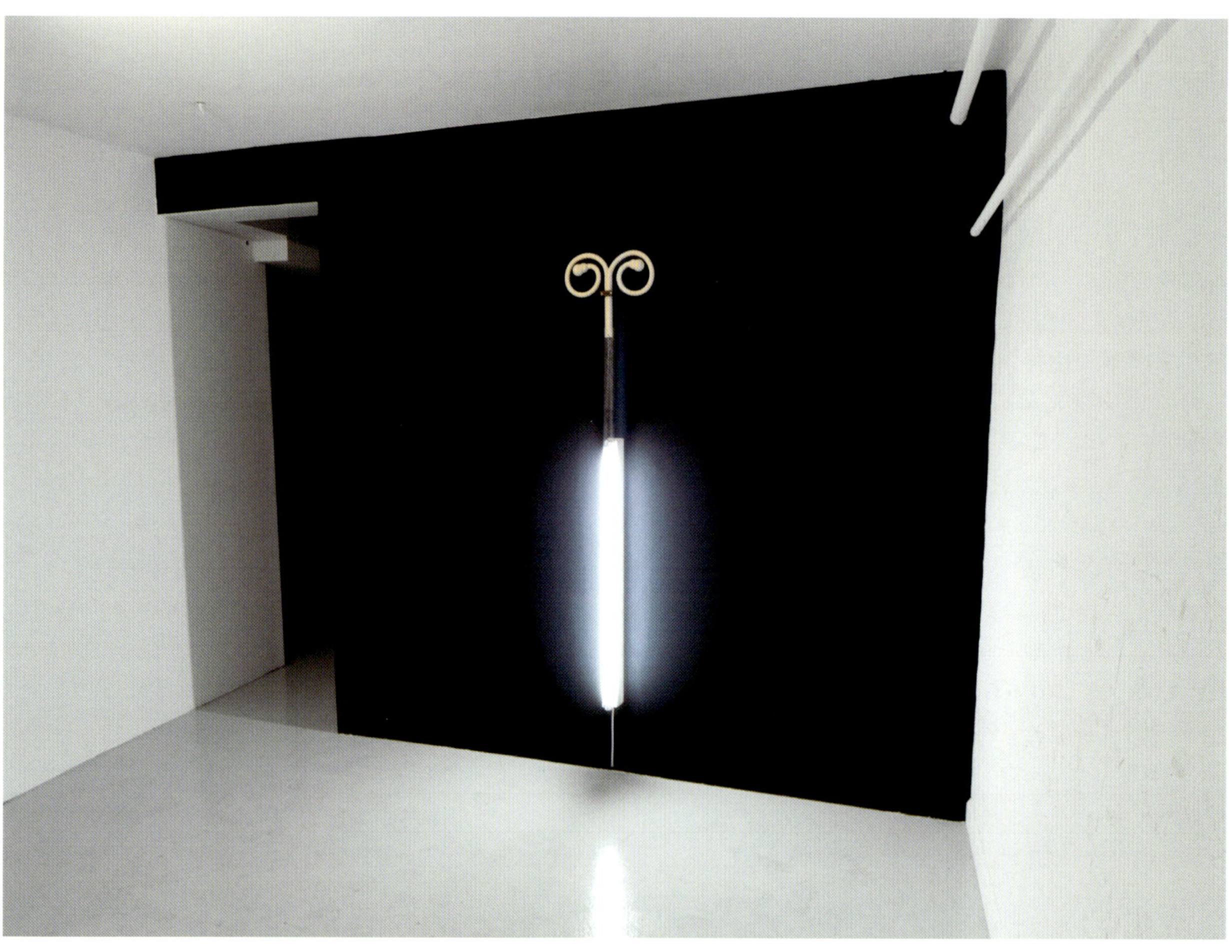

promising to place fifteen chairs in front of a single work of theirs
and convene an audience to stare at it for an hour; or perhaps because an
institution that dedicates the entirety of its resources, space, audience,
and attention to only reflecting on each of their work for six months is not
something they commonly receive.

In 2013, I was offered the opportunity of a new-and-improved context
to develop and pursue these ideas even further—with far greater stability,
infrastructure, and support. The Wattis Institute in San Francisco is not
only another "institute," but also operates under the umbrella of a school,
the California College of the Arts. Once again, I envisioned this institute
as both an exhibition space and research institute. This time, however, the
two functions are kept separate and run parallel to each other: one artist
is "in the gallery," while another is "on our mind." In other words, one
artist receives a production budget to make new work and several thousand
square feet of gallery space to show it, while another artist receives
twelve months of our sustained attention—not in the form of an exhibition,
but a "think tank": a private research group meets monthly, a series of
commissioned essays are published, and a wide range of events take place

Installation view: Rosemarie Trockel, *Spiral Betty*, The
Artist's Institute, 2010

for a general public. In both cases, the emphasis remains on in-depth engagements with individual artists, so as to best focus our attention: for the exhibitions, extensive and repeated studio visits allow conversations about new commissions to slowly evolve and develop over time; and for the "think tank," a small group of art historians, curators, artists, filmmakers, writers, and other professionals convene over the course of an entire year to look at the work of a single artist, think about it, talk about it, read about it, write about it, and relate it to a wider context of art, culture, politics, science, and/or philosophy.

The inaugural year at the Wattis Institute was dedicated to Joan Jonas—we became the Joan Jonas Institute. A year later, we became the Andrea Fraser Institute. Soon, we will become the David Hammons Institute. Over the course of 2014, with Joan Jonas "on our mind" and with specific performances, videos, drawings, and sculptures by the artist as a common point of departure, a research group brought in texts by Ezra Pound, Gilles Deleuze, and Peter Gidal; poems by Susan Howe and David Antin; fairy tales by the Grimm brothers; films by Malcolm Le Grice and Richard Foreman; and YouTube clips of Japanese Noh theater, among many others. Public events featured not only Jonas herself, but also several other visual artists, filmmakers, composers, poets, art historians, and philosophers whose work shares an affinity with Jonas's ideas and concerns—some of them were familiar with Jonas's work while others were not, but each added yet another detour to the elusive task of fully defining the artist's practice. A book will soon be published with newly commissioned texts, descriptions of the many public events, as well as excerpts from readings and reference materials that proved central to the discussions. My hope is that it's a book that Jonas herself will not only enjoy reading, but that will also contain ideas that surprise and inspire her and, who knows, might even inform a future body of work.

This model of attention doesn't aim to explain Jonas, Fraser, or Hammons, or in some way demystify them—quite the opposite. Instead, dedicating an entire year to thinking through their work provides the space for agreements to turn into disagreements and back again. Consensus forms and breaks down in an organic flow of interpretation, speculation, critique, and debate. Clarifications and contradictions both have time to accumulate, and neither quite cancels out the other. A range of other artists and ideas, when gradually brought into contact with the work over the course of a year, causes overlaps to occur and differences to emerge, and the friction this generates inevitably complicates and animates the work in new ways. By the end of each year, I hope to understand Jonas's, Fraser's, or Hammons's work less than I did when we began.

The initial concept for the Artist's Institute and the Wattis Institute had come from a reflection on what an "institute" might mean and how it could offer a possible alternative to today's existing models of the art museum, the *kunsthalle*, the commercial gallery, the artist-run space—or at least suggest a specificity in approach and position that was in tune with the concerns of many artists. Many museums obviously keep the same works on view for years at a time in the context of their permanent collection, but few demand the same attention for their temporary exhibitions. However, a range of other organizations are placing an emphasis on sustained attention, although they differ in size, mission, and location.

For decades, the Dia Art Foundation in New York has had the habit of keeping its temporary shows on view for approximately eight months and encouraging repeated visits—it once even presented three consecutive Thomas Schütte shows. BAK in Utrecht and If I Can't Dance in Amsterdam both dedicate several years to investigating a single theme via exhibitions, conferences, publications, performances, reading groups, workshops, and other itinerant events. Mamco in Geneva often returns to the same artists to show their work a second or even a third time over the course of several years. Yale Union in Portland always puts the demands of the work first, and should an exhibition not make sense in its own galleries, but only in a nearby theater or under a nearby bridge, then they simply close their space and leave it empty. The Artist's Institute, now running under the leadership of Jaskey, is no longer showing just a single work at a time, but commissioning several successive and distinct installations by the same artist over the course of each six-month season, making its commitment to their work even more pronounced. Other nonprofit alternative spaces in New York, such as Cage or the Emily Harvey Foundation, embrace the productive nature of the semiprivate, keep no regular hours, and choose to be open only to an engaged audience who makes appointments.

This wide range of large, small, rich, and not-rich organizations doesn't fit into what is usually considered "alternative," and thereby implies that the term, which has lost many of the teeth it once had in the 1970s, could benefit from a new set of parameters. In a context where the marketplace quickly accommodates its own critique, and where powerful dealers and art advisors sit on the boards of the most critically minded nonprofits, how do we begin to redefine and rearticulate what it means to occupy an alternative position today, or to identify a role that commercial galleries and larger museums either can't or won't play? When the terms "experimental," "innovative," "emerging," and "challenging the status quo" now appear on nearly every billboard between San Francisco and Silicon Valley, their status as indicators of an alternative position has become problematic. Instead, the approaches outlined above construct specific models of attention, narrowing their focus, and suggest an alternative to expansion-happy and audience-hungry museums, fast-paced and blog-friendly *kunsthalles* or artist-run spaces, and commerce-driven art galleries. Instead, they pay attention to the work itself, respecting the time it demands from its viewers, and require that an audience meet it on its own terms: "Chapter one. In my younger and more vulnerable years, my father gave me some advice that I've been turning over in my mind ever since [...]"

A version of this essay was originally printed in: frieze, *No. 172 (June—August 2015), 146.*

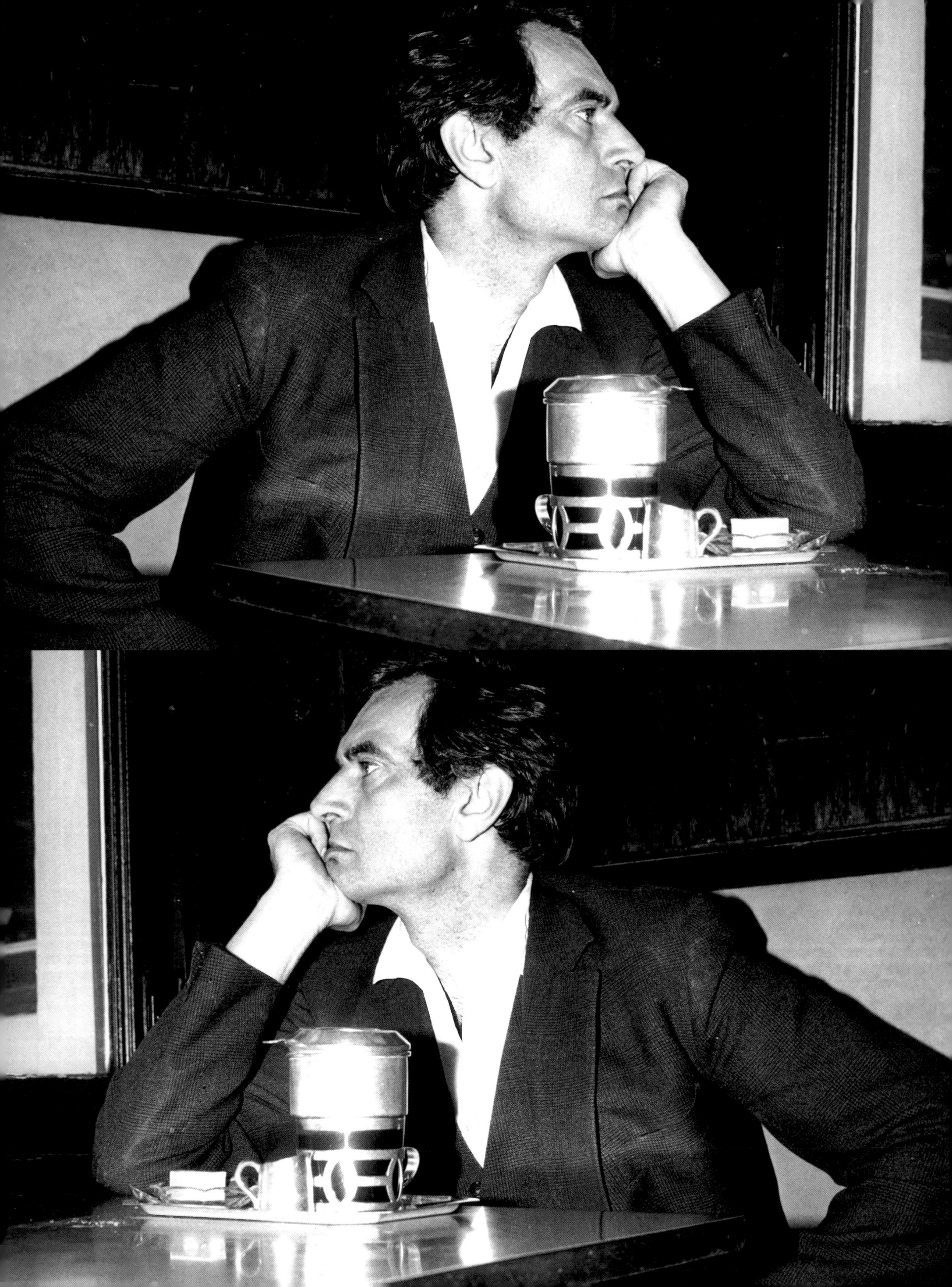

Interview with Marcel Broodthaers by Marcel Broodthaers

Interviewer "My dear sir, concerning your letter dated the 12th of this month, which says that you intend to publish a catalogue of my exhibition, I would like my biography to be published at the same time, because this conveys the diversity of structures in which I have been active. I would suggest that you also reproduce the medical certificate that is exhibited with my drawings, and the one that appears in the catalogue of the exhibition *18 Paris IV.70*. It is important to me that these two certificates, and these two exhibitions, should be compared. Yours faithfully. Marcel Broodthaers."

This is the opening of the catalogue to an exhibition held in Brussels last month. An exhibition by Marcel Broodthaers who is here with us now. We are going to ask him about his intentions and about the reasons behind this exhibition featuring the medical certificates. Marcel Broodthaers, what are the main moments in your biography, which you mention in the letter addressed to the publisher of your catalogue?

Marcel Broodthaers I was born on 28-1-24, in Brussels, Belgium, where I live and work. First cultural and public option in 1949. In 1958, I presented a film on Kurt Schwitters, 7'–16 mm, at the festival of experimental film, at Knokke. My activity during this period is fragmentary and discontinued. It becomes regular in 1964.

I In what way, Mr Broodthaers, did this date of 1964 determine a regular activity?

MB My activity has been regular since 1964. I think that is the important point.

I I note that your catalogue is printed in French, in Flemish, and in English. Why these different languages, Mr. Broodthaers?

MB That was the wish of the director of the gallery that put on the exhibition. The wish of Mr Fernand Spillemaeckers, who runs Galerie MTL. I agreed to this idea because I think it's useful, especially in artistic matters, to address oneself, to make maximum use of the means of communication given us by languages. I think this is perfectly natural, especially since the town where I live is bilingual, at least from the administrative viewpoint.

I Yes, and in fact, the same formula was used in the catalogue for the exhibition in Paris in which you also took part, wasn't it?

MB Yes, you must be referring to the exhibition organized by Michel Claura and Seth Siegelaub at 66, Rue Mouffetard, bringing together eighteen English, American, Dutch, and other artists. Is that it?

I Yes.

MB But there the three languages are French, German, and English. I think it's a very good idea, too, that.

I I read in the catalogue, in the pages set aside for you, I read, Mr Broodthaers: "Reminder of what the Musée d'Art Moderne, my own, was, i.e., a décor made up of packing crates, postcards, and inscriptions, etc. Projection of a film." In short, you describe a project, which is in fact illustrated by two photos representing a map of the world, with the word "Museum" printed over them.

I went to this exhibition, which I must say surprised me greatly, because there was hardly anything to see. It was an exhibition that expressed itself through ideas, concepts, projects. Then I read a letter you sent to the organizer in which you are withdrawing from this museum project claiming that a medical certificate will explain the reason for this non-undertaking. This certificate states that your health requires no special treatment and that you can go back to work as normal. It is dated 15 January, 1970.

I would therefore like to ask you the following question: did you use this as an excuse for giving visitors to this exhibition nothing to look at? Why did you send a medical certificate and not show anything?

MB Look, first of all, I would like to tell you that I like this exhibition very much and the organizers really made a very special effort with the presentation, and with being honest, too. Personally, I think it's a fine exhibition. As for your question, I find it indiscreet and really do not wish to answer it.

I Ah, look, Mr Broodthaers, I ask you this question because I note that in the catalogue for the exhibition you have just finished in Brussels, there is also a medical certificate that says almost the opposite. It's a certificate from a doctor specializing in nervous conditions. This certificate says that this time your state of health makes you unfit for any normal professional activity. You will understand that I feel justified in putting this question to you again: Is there a relation between the medical certificate published in your catalogue and the fact that in this exhibition in Brussels you have shown lots of pieces, I mean, manuscripts and drawings?

MB Look, I have simply availed myself of my freedom to publish medical certificates. And this freedom has nothing to do with

either the doctors who wrote them
or the exhibition organizers.

I Look, Mr Broodthaers, I don't
mean to insist, but it seems to me
that there is a connection between
these certificates, the fact of a
special sort of space, which is that
of the exhibitions, I mean that
all these things are connected. But
since you apparently do not wish
to discuss this subject, I shall
ask you another question, if you
will. Your exhibition in Brussels
looks like a graphic arts collection.
The catalogue actually describes
it in great detail: "Capital A.
Description of the first part..."

   Further down, I read: "The
exhibition also included, on
the gallery window and legible
only from inside, an inscription
repeating the text of the
invitation," and further on, in the
form of an addendum, corrections
and also changes: "The idea of
replacing the inscription with
a biographical summary became
superfluous for the following
reason: when the catalogue was
going to press, the artist was able
to concretize an initial project,
that is to say, to make a film
about the letters composing the
inscription on the window." Don't
you agree, Mr Broodthaers that this
is all extremely complicated?...

   Capital C. Description of the
   third part...
   Capital D. Description of the
   fourth part. Sixteen pieces
   in a folder with the same
   characteristics...

Tell me, Mr Broodthaers, tell me,
what are these characteristics?

MB Er, yes, if you want, although
I'm not very keen. Well, *L'Appeau*, if
you like.

I Ah, yes, certainly, *L'Appeau*. An
appeau, I believe, is the decoy used
in hunting to trick the hunted
animal, to lure it before the
hunter's gun.

MB Yes, that's it exactly. *L'Appeau*.
Capital nightmare. Capital itself.
Foreign poems bought here. Object
anxiety. Love anxiety. Invisible
anxiety.

I Ah, thank you, that's very good.
So here Capital plays the role of
the object used to trick the animal
and lure it before the hunter's gun.
What do you think of Capital, Mr
Broodthaers?

MB Well, I think that when I
wrote this poem, I had the highest
possible opinion of Capital. It
enabled me to make a foreign poem,
to sell anxiety, object anxiety, love
anxiety, invisible anxiety.

I So this decoy appears in your
catalogue in the form of a title
under the number 8, I think, in the
Capital C part of your piece.

MB Oh, no no no, sir, you are
mistaken. Under number 8 appears
Le Charcutier, manuscript, deletion,
and graffiti.

I Oh, excuse me. Let's start again then, if you don't mind.... *L'Appeau* is in fact number 15 in the description of your catalogue under the letter Capital C. May I read this text again?

MB Yes, yes, if you like. Yes, go ahead.

I Capital nightmare. Capital itself. Foreign poems bought here. Object anxiety. Love anxiety. Invisible anxiety.

I can, in fact, see a deletion in pencil, but a deletion concerning the sentence written below: "The most bourgeois thing for a boa, is to think of itself as a snake." Tell me, Mr Broodthaers, is this a text to be read or a picture to be looked at?

MB A picture, of course, as the catalogue says. This picture is described under the Capital C. Description of the third part...

I Thank you. Your catalogue also contains a very detailed biography. Do you like biographies, Mr Broodthaers?

MB Yes, quite a lot. Listen: Group events and exhibitions, in '65, the *Comparaisons* salon, in Paris. *La Leçon de choses*, Paris. In '66, Galerie Pilote, with the New Smith Gallery, in Antwerp. In '68, at the same gallery, *Le Corbeau et le Renard*, in Kassel. *Prospekt 68*, in Düsseldorf. *Three Blind Mice* in Eindhoven. In '69, *Language III* at the Dwan Gallery, in New York. The Stedelijk Van Abbemuseum, in Eindhoven. The Bruges Triennale. *The Forum d'art graphique*, in Ghent. *Conception*, in Leverkusen. *Le Corbeau et le Renard*, in Cologne. In '70, *Between*, at the Düsseldorf Kunsthalle. *Mÿn Dorado*, at the Middelheim, in Antwerp. And *18 Paris IV.70*, in Paris. Yes I do find biography pleasant. It's rather nice to have done something, isn't it, to show it, to make it known to people, don't you think?

I *Le Corbeau et le Renard*, in Kassel, what was that?

MB Ah, *Le Corbeau et le Renard*. It is figured under the letter small b in subdivision number 3 of the piece that is described in the catalogue, under the letter Capital A. Master Crow, up high on a tree perched so, a piece of cheese gripped in his beak. In the following tones to him did speak: Well good day to you, sir my good Lord Crow. How pretty you seem, and how handsome you know. To be sure, if your warblage is a match for your plumage, you're the Phoenix of all who dwell in this wood. At these words, the crow feels no joy, and to reveal his beautiful voice, he opened wide his beak and dropped his prey. The Fox snapped it up and said: My good sir, learn that all flatterers live at the expense of those who heed their words. This lesson is surely worth a cheese. The Crow, ashamed and confused, swore, though rather late, that he would not be deceived again. (Music from a music box.)

I Yes, that's very nice music,
Mr Broodthaers.

MB But no, sir, this is a painting.

I A painting.

MB *L'Appeau*. Capital nightmare.
Capital itself. Foreign poems
bought here. Object anxiety. Love
anxiety. Invisible anxiety.
    The letter capital D. The capital
D is bigger than the capital T. All
capital Ds should be of the same
length. The downstroke and the
oval have the same slope as the
capital A. Model: the dog. the fox.
Koekelberg. the cries. the hands.
the orchid. the architect. the feet.
the hands. Paris, the deceitfulness,
the voices, the cries, the character,
the print, the print, the agora.
the blue. the red. the... Making
objects, social activity, revise
the text, logic of illuminations,
outskirts, gas, hands, the wild
gentlemen, the coffee cup, mussels,
current artistic epoch, galleries,
collectors, artists, mussels, eggs,
bricks, canvases, spider, molding,
prefabricated, deletion, theoretical
vision, deletion. for spectator,
deletion, papers, magazines,
assignees, photography, natural,
sky, note, photo. What'll. What one.
Photo. Image on canvas. Theory
without color. Logical theory.
Theory of money. Theory. Morality.
Theory. Modern art. Added value
in authentic conditions. Memory.
Memory. Memory...

I I read further on, Mr Broodthaers,
in the form of an addendum number
3, the following letter:

Dear Sir,
    I am happy to hear that you
have sold the piece in four parts,
Capital A, Capital B, Capital C,
and Capital D, described in the
exhibition catalogue. I should
tell you, however, that I thought
you would; indeed, in order to
expedite your commerce, I have
made a personal transaction with
your customer. This transaction
concerned a case that you know
well, the very one that was headed
for the bin when, after much
procrastination—I had to find in
my reserves an artistic ensemble
that was perplexing enough to
illustrate the medical certificate
attesting incapacity for work—we
chose it and removed from it these
manuscripts and these drawings. It
so happens, then, that my intention
to constitute a single piece
including manuscripts and drawings,
an inscription on a window, a film
on this inscription, was respected
by your buyer. Is it not natural,
then, that this case, which still
contains the residue we chose,
should also be considered a part of
my undertaking? May I suggest, dear
sir, that you publish this letter and
print in red the words: this piece is
part of the exhibition.

Yours, etc.
✳

First published in: Marcel
Broodthaers: Cinéma *(Barcelona:*
Fundació Antoni Tàpies, 1997),
110–111. EN: Transcription from
an audiotape on which Broodthaers
interviews himself.

Simon Denny

Secret Power: Unpacking Original Visual Content in the Snowden NSA Slides

This slideshow summarizes my process in unpacking the images released through Edward Snowden's leaks of NSA and related security agency internal slides and memos. This research became the core of my pavilion representing New Zealand at the Venice Biennale in 2015.

A close partner with the USA, New Zealand is also a support figure to America in intelligence matters—a part of the "Five Eyes" alliance of intelligence agencies, including the US, UK, Canada, Australia, and New Zealand. In finding and engaging one of the designers responsible for many of the images used and produced internally in the NSA, my hope was to apply cultural tools to help understand some of the values inside the usually closed world of government intelligence agencies.

To me, the NSA slides contain some of the most retroactively powerful, far-reaching images produced in the contemporary moment, and to treat them as such, using the tools of art, might be a way to digest that power.

NSA symbolizes data-collection program with wizard

This is a cover slide from a weekly briefing slide deck from the NSA's Special Source Operations team, responsible for deploying and maintaining bulk collection methods. Read more about the NSA surveillance program

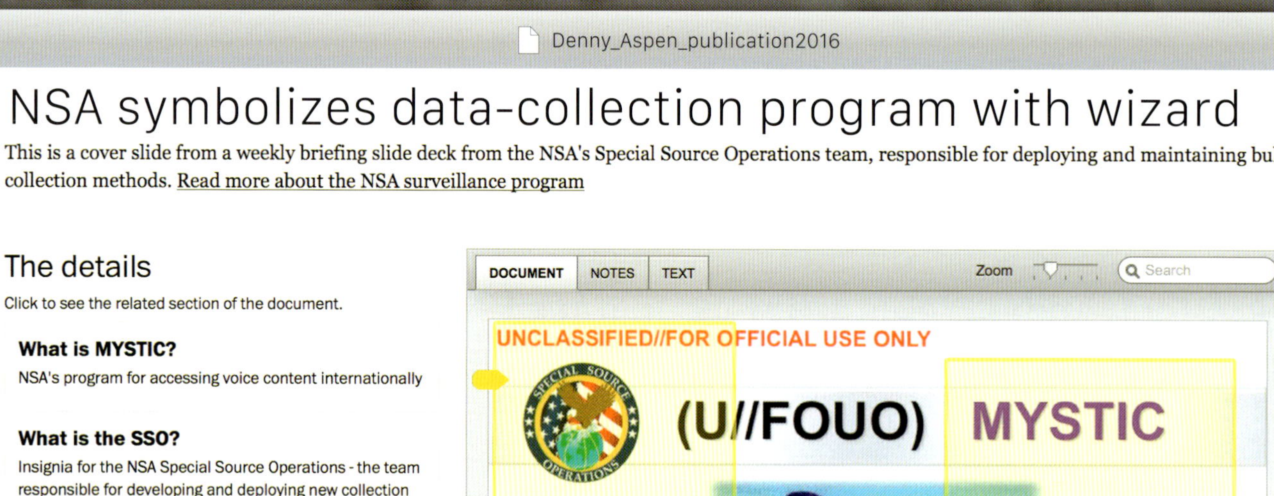

Edward Snowden's 2013 leaks of internal documents from the National Security Agency contained many images. These images gave me a sublime feeling when I first viewed them. They outlined a contemporary visual language for imaging power and secrecy. Ironic, provocative, and interned for a group of private eyes, this tone contrasted with the reach and gravity of their subject matter—making something truly affecting. Far from simply "trashy" or "badly designed," as the design community seemed to view them, to me, the images were a rich source of information about the logic of intelligence communities and their organizational culture.

Appropriated images used in NSA slides

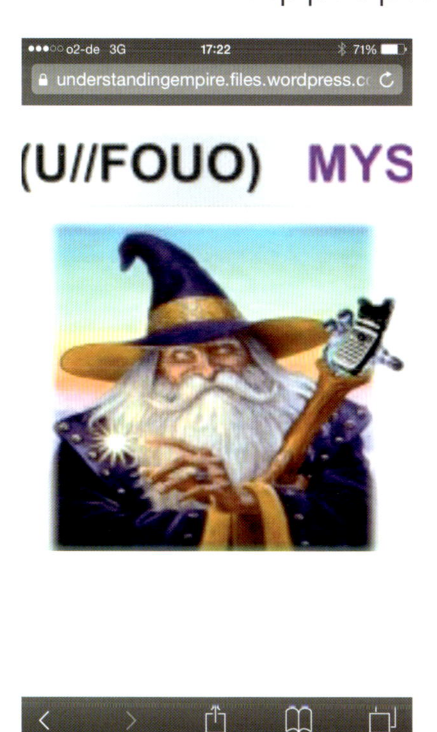

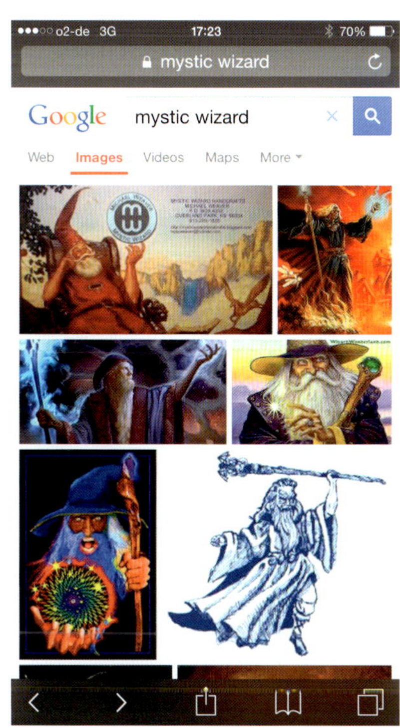

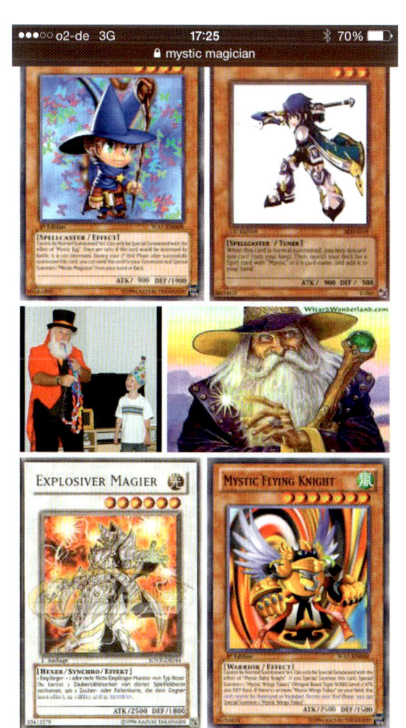

The documents contained a mix of appropriation and original images. When borrowing imagery from other sources, the way they were used was very similar to the way people use images on forums like 4chan or even Facebook—taken from diverse contexts across the web that could be easily found with quick Google searches. Here, the source for the "Mystic Wizard" collage in the NSA's "Mystic" slide is found in two quick Google searches as one of the top results, underlining its ubiquity on the wider internet.

Appropriated images used in NSA slides

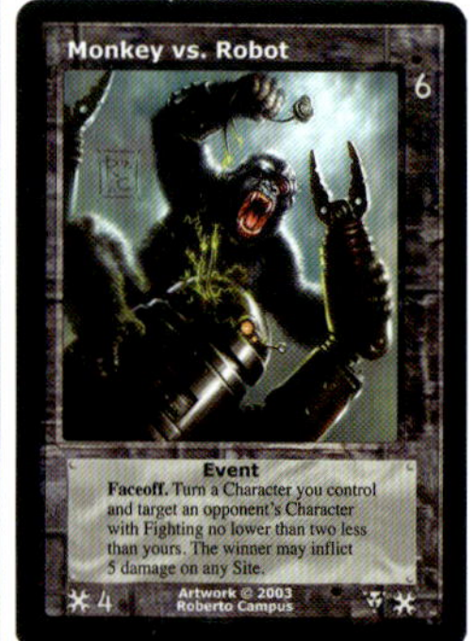
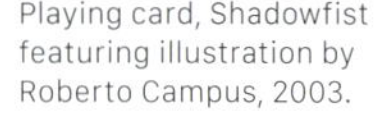

Playing card, Shadowfist featuring illustration by Roberto Campus, 2003.

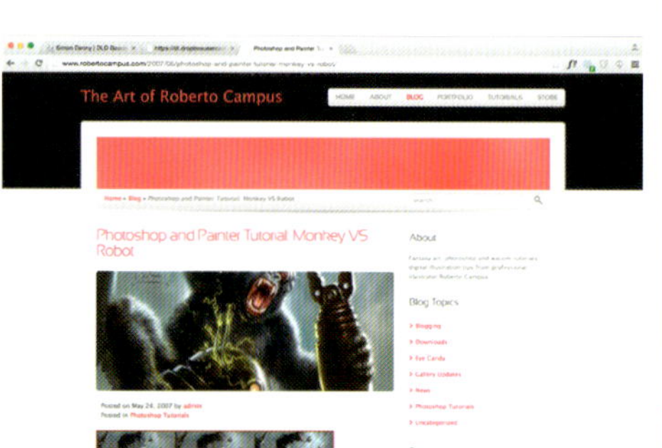

'The Art of Roberto Campo' website.

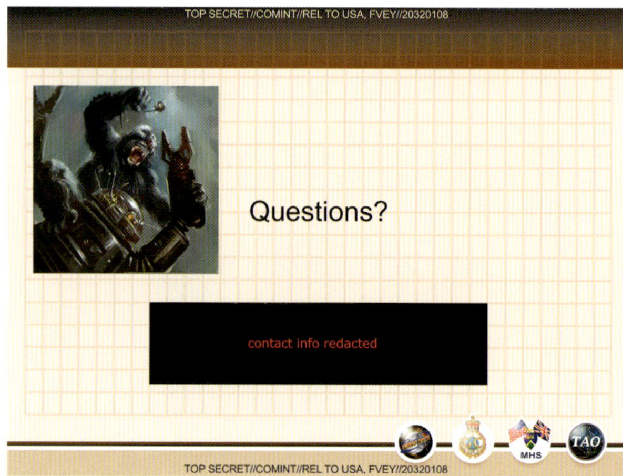

NSA slide, QUANTUMTHEORY program, published The Intercept, 12 March 2014.

Many slides used imagery from games or a sci-fi/fantasy context. This "Shadowfist" fantasy card game image (similar to the very popular Magic: the Gathering) by artist Roberto Campus was used to illustrate the NSA's "Quantumtheory" surveillance program.

NSA-generated images used in NSA slides

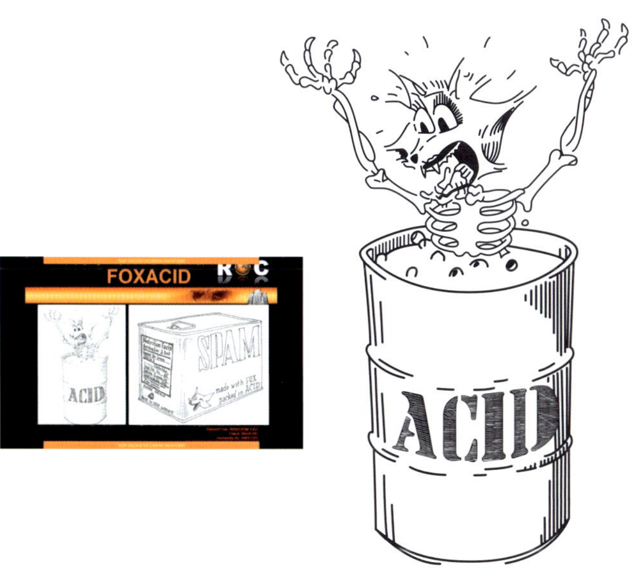
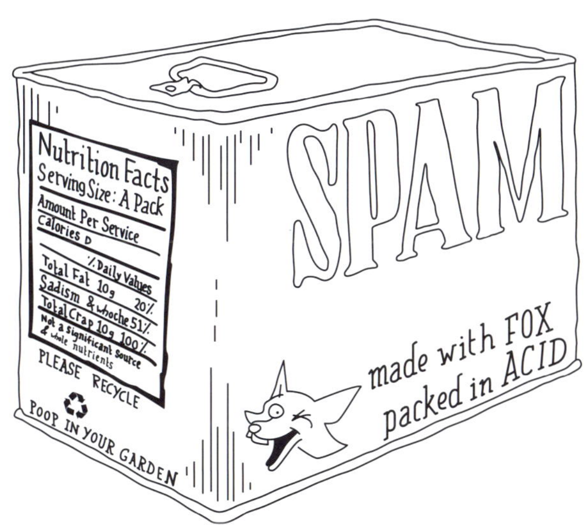

The original imagery (illustrations not found outside the slides) was more complex and interesting. Here, one of the most amazing drawings from the "Foxacid" slide deck features a fox screaming while drowning in a barrel of acid and a spam can's ingredients listed as "51% Sadism" and "100% Total Crap."

NSA-generated images used in NSA slides

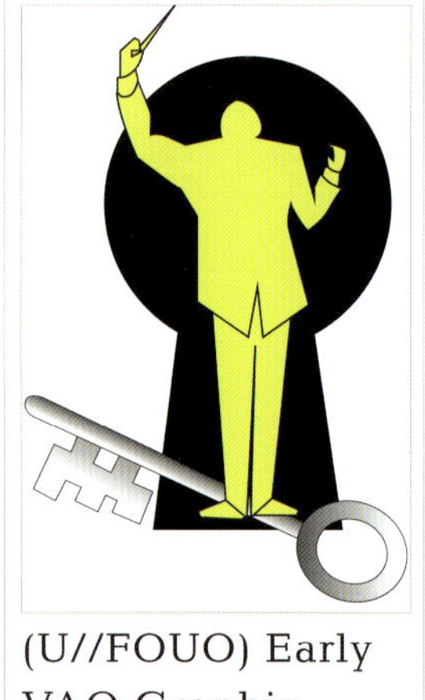

(U//FOUO) Early VAO Graphic

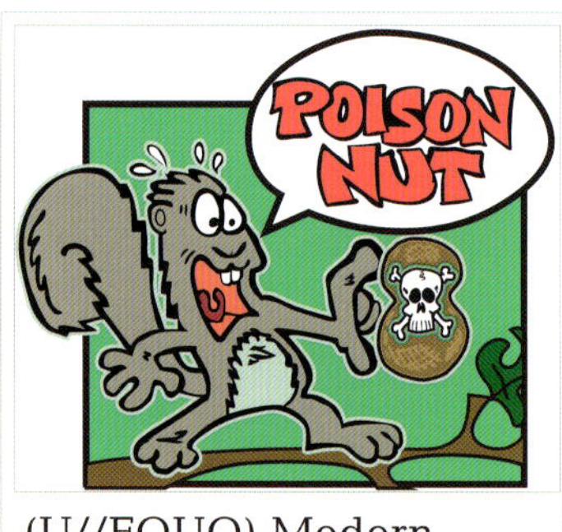

(U//FOUO) Modern POISONNUT Graphic

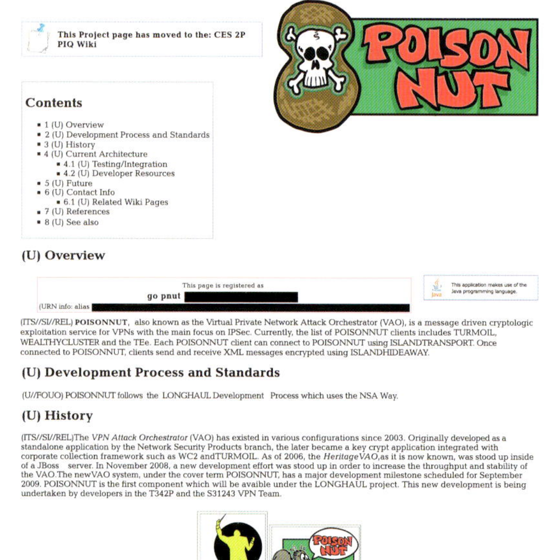

POISONNUT - WikiInfo

The accredited security level of this system is TOP SECRET//SI-GAMMA/TALENT KEYHOLE//ORCON/PROPIN/RELIDO/REL TO USA, FVEY •
TOP SECRET//SI/REL TO USA, FVEY   (U) POISONNUT Adminibar:

(S//REL) POISONNUT

This Project page has moved to the: CES 2P PIQ Wiki

Contents

- 1 (U) Overview
- 2 (U) Development Process and Standards
- 3 (U) History
- 4 (U) Current Architecture
  - 4.1 (U) Testing/Integration
  - 4.2 (U) Developer Resources
- 5 (U) Future
- 6 (U) Contact Info
  - 6.1 (U) Related Wiki Pages
- 7 (U) References
- 8 (U) See also

(U) Overview

This page is registered as
go pnut
(URN info: alias

This application makes use of the Java programming language.

(TS//SI//REL) **POISONNUT**, also known as the Virtual Private Network Attack Orchestrator (VAO), is a message driven cryptologic exploitation service for VPNs with the main focus on IPSec. Currently, the list of POISONNUT clients includes TURMOIL, WEALTHYCLUSTER and the TEe. Each POISONNUT client can connect to POISONNUT using ISLANDTRANSPORT. Once connected to POISONNUT, clients send and receive XML messages encrypted using ISLANDHIDEAWAY.

(U) Development Process and Standards

(U//FOUO) POISONNUT follows the LONGHAUL Development   Process which uses the NSA Way.

(U) History

(TS//SI//REL)The *VPN Attack Orchestrator* (VAO) has existed in various configurations since 2003. Originally developed as a standalone application by the Network Security Products branch, the later became a key crypt application integrated with corporate collection framework such as WC2 andTURMOIL. As of 2006, the *Heritage VAO,*as it is now known, was stood up inside of a JBoss   server. In November 2008, a new development effort was stood up in order to increase the throughput and stability of the VAO.The newVAO system, under the cover term POISONNUT, has a major development milestone scheduled for September 2009. POISONNUT is the first component which will be avaible under the LONGHAUL project. This new development is being undertaken by developers in the T342P and the S31243 VPN Team.

(U//FOUO) Early VAO Graphic

(U//FOUO) Modern POISONNUT Graphic

(U) Current Architecture

1 of 2

6

This document describing the "Poisonnut" VPN attack program showed an unusual detail: an evolution of a logo for the program over time. The conductor and keyhole image was made obsolete when a squirrel with a skull-bearing peanut replaced it.

7

8

9

10

11

12

13

14

15

16

17

18

19

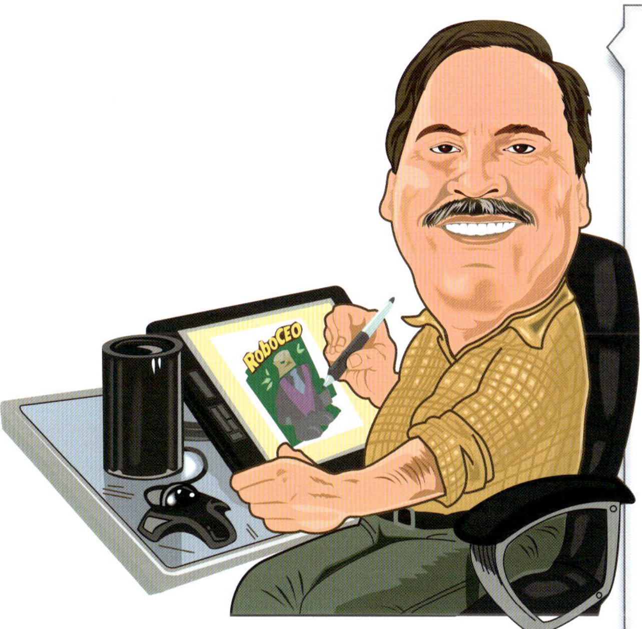

This is a redrawn self-portrait of David Darchicourt, an amazing artist I came across through social media while looking for a way to understand the artistic context of the original images that were released as part of the Snowden archive. To his right, excerpts from his LinkedIn profile describe his position as Creative Director of the NSA from 2001–12. To the left, a logo for the VPN tracking program "Poisonnut," which I found in a 2014 release through *Der Spiegel*.

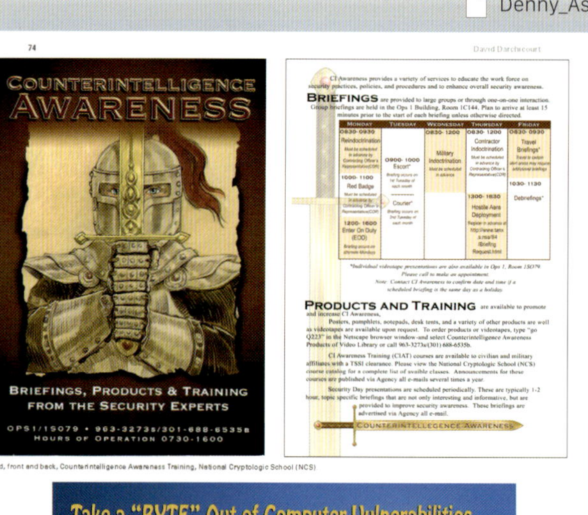

Card, front and back, Counterintelligence Awareness Training, National Cryptologic School (NCS)

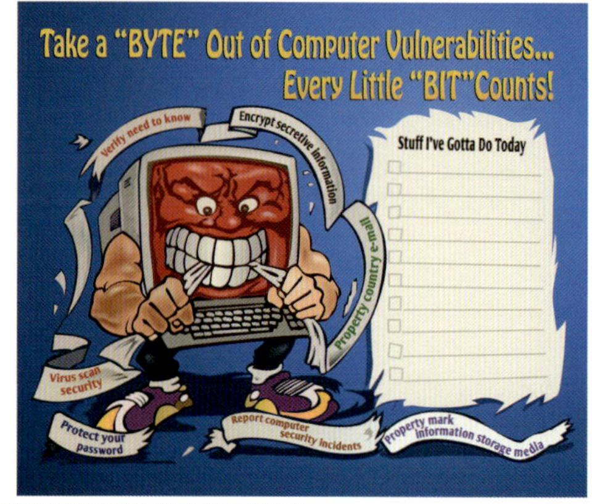

Mousepad. Redrawn by Mahmoud Sayed, Cairo, commissioned through Freelancer.com.

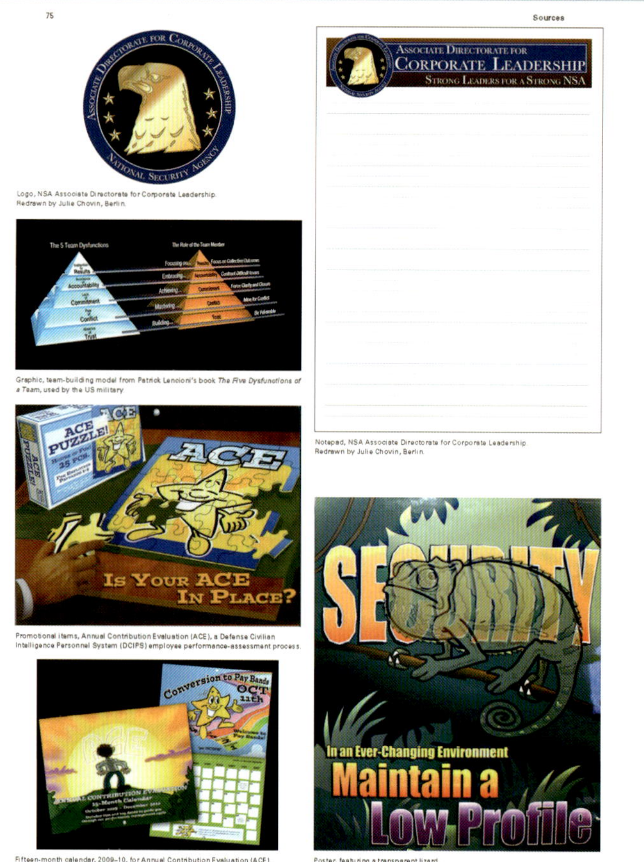

Logo, NSA Associate Directorate for Corporate Leadership. Redrawn by Julie Chovin, Berlin.

Graphic, team-building model from Patrick Lencioni's book *The Five Dysfunctions of a Team*, used by the US military.

Promotional items, Annual Contribution Evaluation (ACE), a Defense Civilian Intelligence Personnel System (DCIPS) employee performance-assessment process.

Fifteen-month calendar, 2009–10, for Annual Contribution Evaluation (ACE).

Notepad, NSA Associate Directorate for Corporate Leadership. Redrawn by Julie Chovin, Berlin.

Poster, featuring a transparent lizard.

His public profile on Adobe's freelancer platform, Behance, fleshed out the Snowden original drawings—and NSA organizational culture—in ways I couldn't have expected. From management strategies, like Patrick Lencioni's popular book *The Five Dysfunctions of a Team*, to animated performance review posters, information security training programs, and reminders of extreme secrecy.

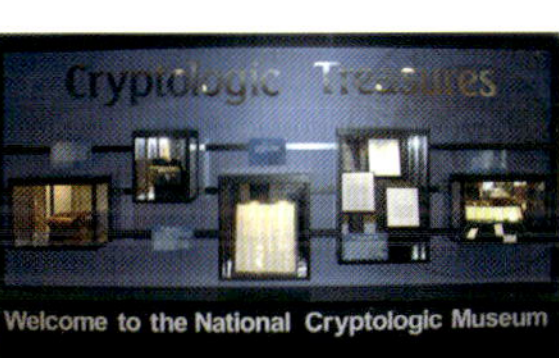

'Cryptologic Treasures', exhibition design, National Cryptologic Museum.

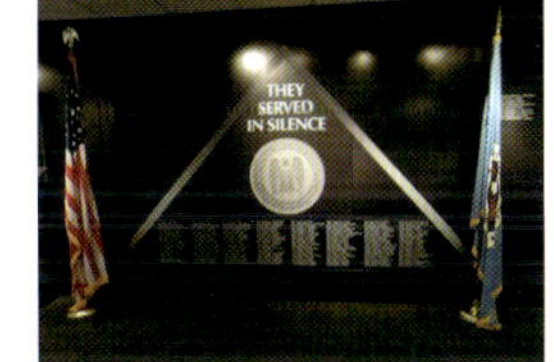

Memorial to 173 cryptologists who lost their lives in service, NSA headquarters, adjacent to the National Cryptologic Museum.

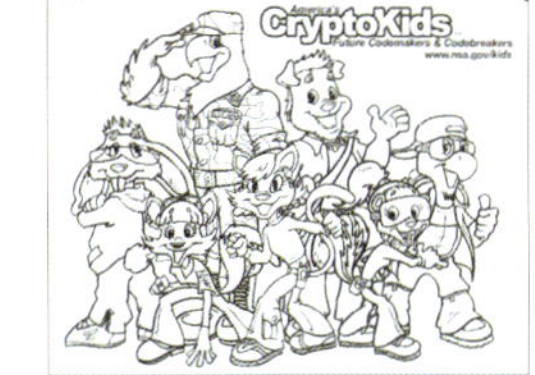

Colouring-in page, *CryptoKids Fun Book*.

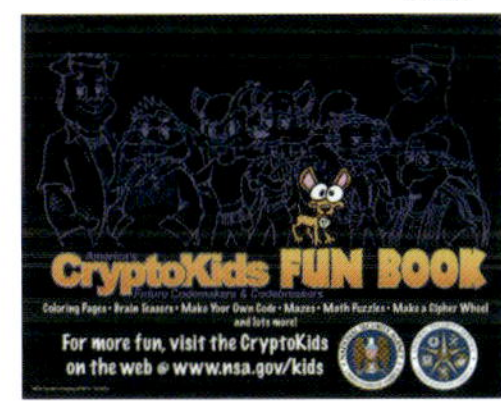

Back cover, *CryptoKids Fun Book*, features NSA and CSS seals.

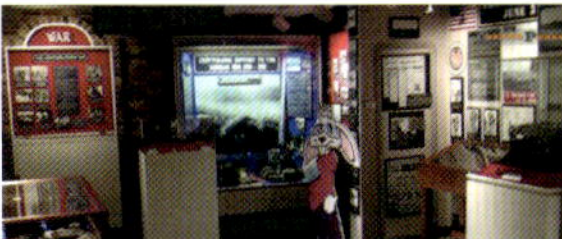

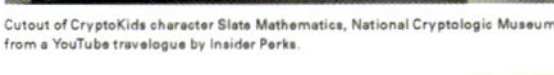

Cutout of CryptoKids character Slate Mathematics, National Cryptologic Museum, from a YouTube travelogue by Insider Perks.

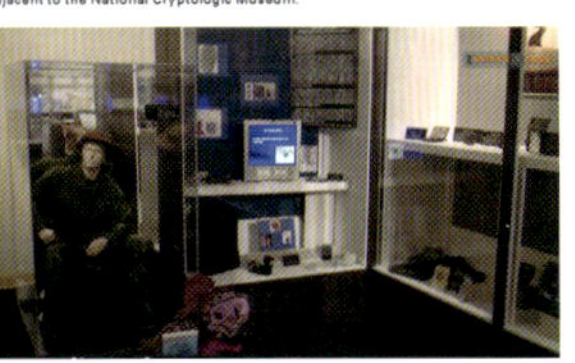

Cutout of CryptoKids character Joules the Engineer, National Cryptologic Museum, from a YouTube travelogue by Insider Perks.

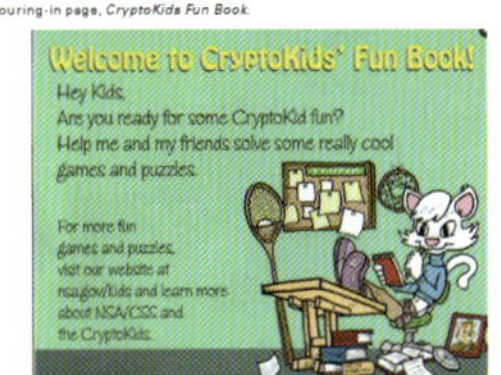

Welcome page, *CryptoKids Fun Book*, features Crypto Cat.

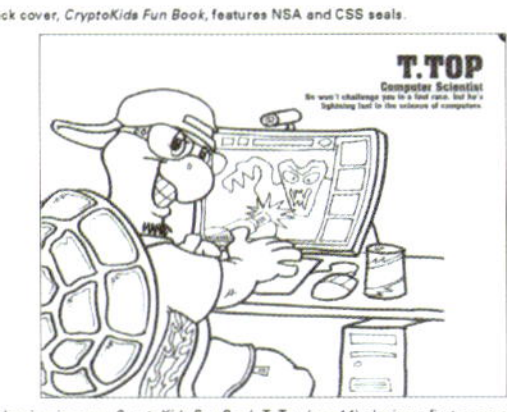

Colouring-in page, *CryptoKids Fun Book*. T. Top (age 14) playing a first-person-shooter (FPS) computer game.

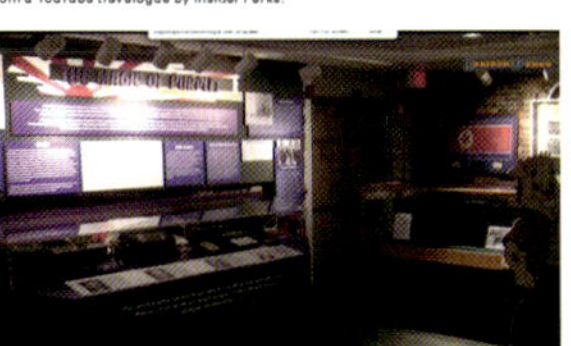

'The Magic of Purple', exhibition design, National Cryptologic Museum. This display addresses the deciphering of Japan's diplomatic ciphers during World War II. From a YouTube travelogue by Insider Perks.

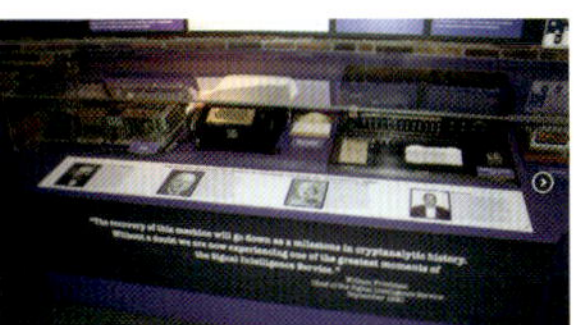

'The Magic of Purple', exhibition design, National Cryptologic Museum. From a YouTube travelogue by Insider Perks.

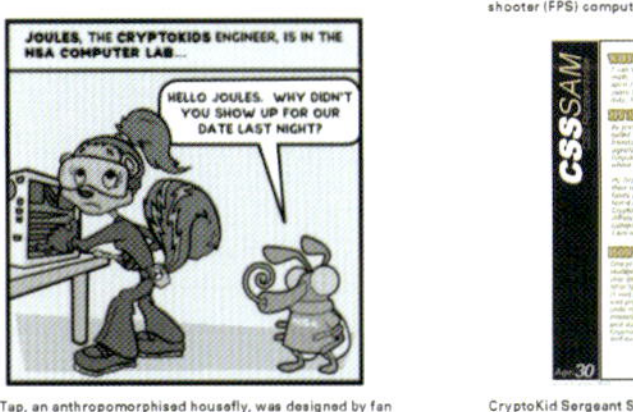

CryptoKid Y.R. Tap, an anthropomorphised housefly, was designed by fan Lyle Zapato. Tap made his way into National Cryptologic Museum internal newsletters. Here he surprises Joules the Engineer.

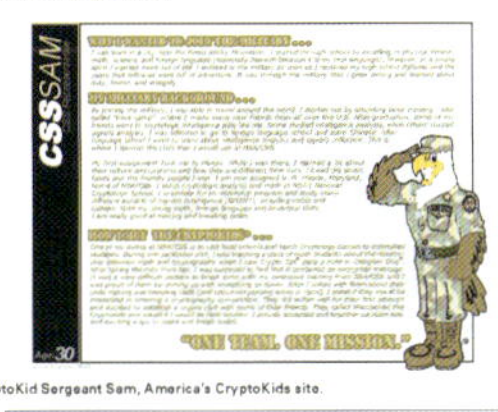

CryptoKid Sergeant Sam, America's CryptoKids site.

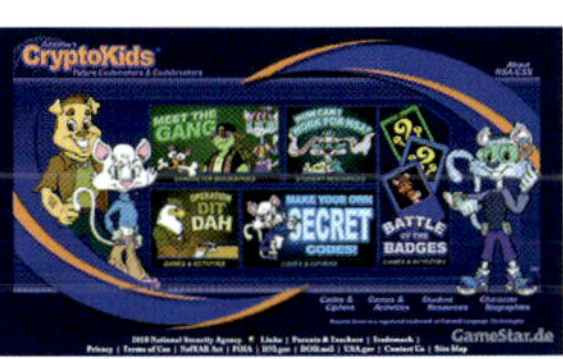

NSA, America's *CryptoKids Future Codemakers and Codebreakers*, home page.

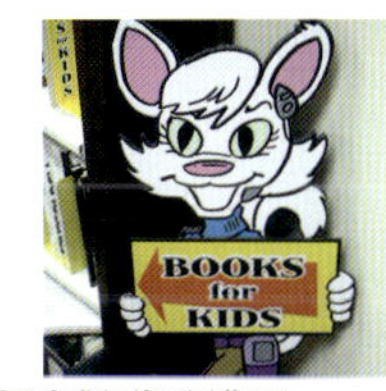

Cutout of Crypto Cat, National Cryptologic Museum.

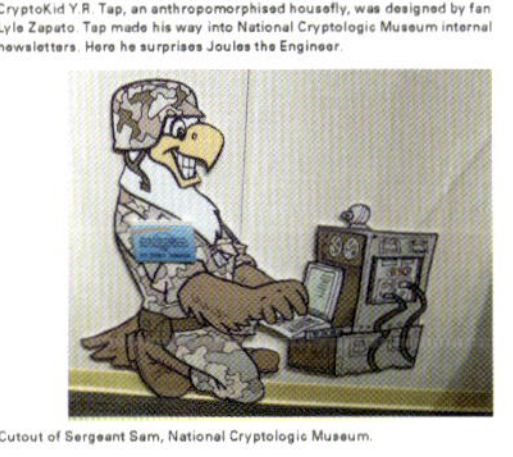

Cutout of Sergeant Sam, National Cryptologic Museum.

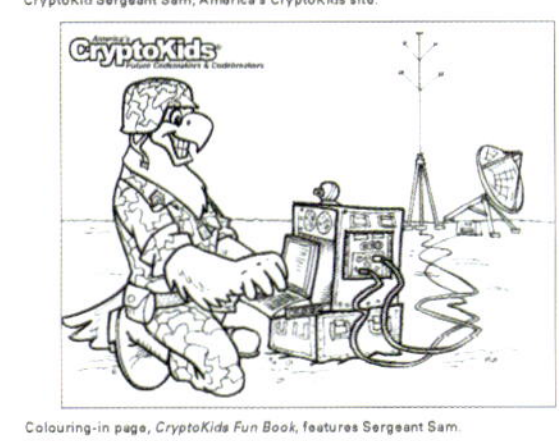

Colouring-in page, *CryptoKids Fun Book*, features Sergeant Sam.

9

Even exhibition and public program designs for the NSA's own public-facing museum—the National Cryptographic Museum (NCM)—were featured in the portfolio. These included amazing displays with a high information density and playful cartoon guides for children—in a similar visual hand to many of the drawings in the Snowden-leaked slides.

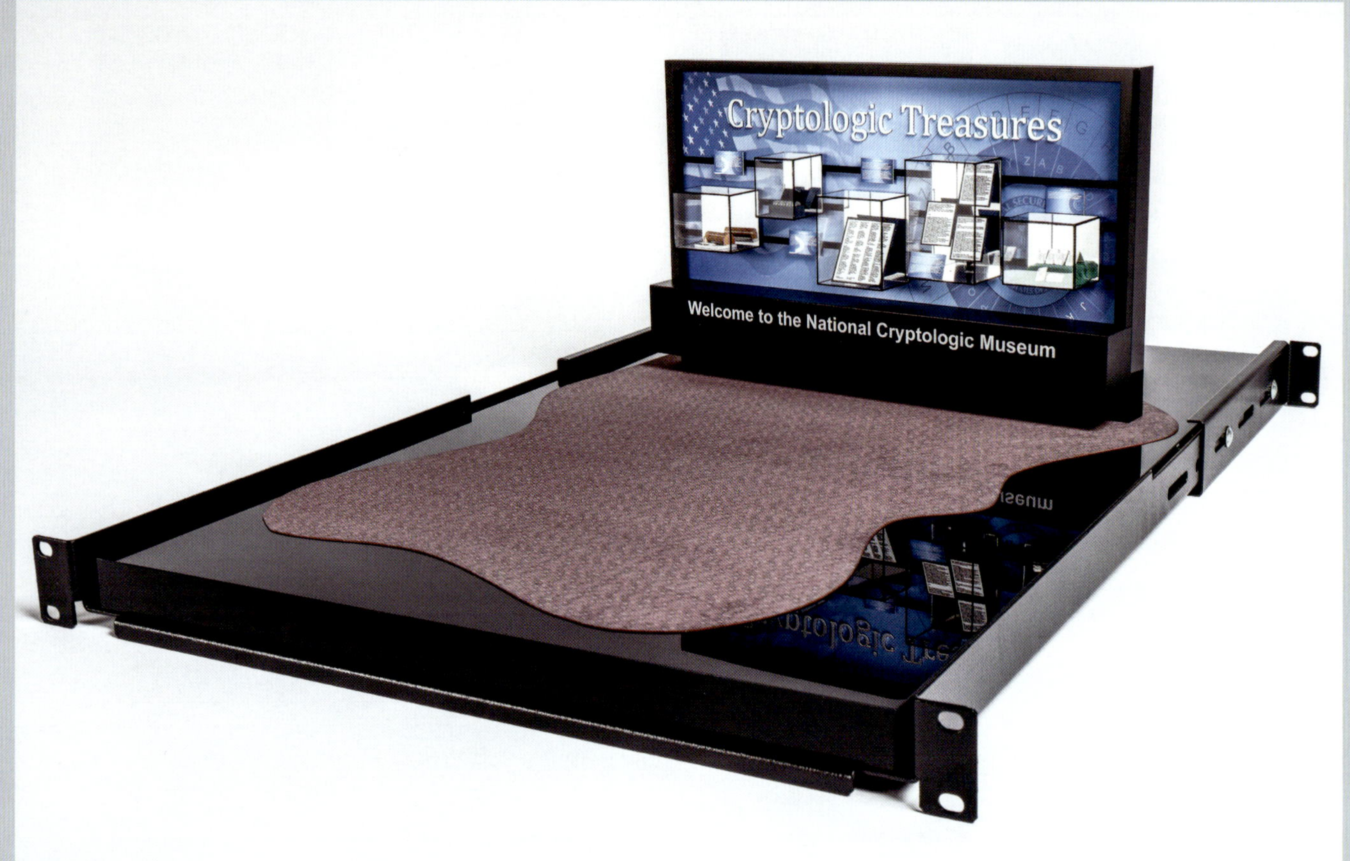

To gather and monumentalize the importance of the material and position of Darchicourt as Creative Director and possible author of the slide imagery, I mimicked some of these display strategies and mixed them with data storage computer hardware to create hybrid sculptural summaries of the NSA's aesthetic terrain. This depicts one of those displays I had reproduced in miniature.

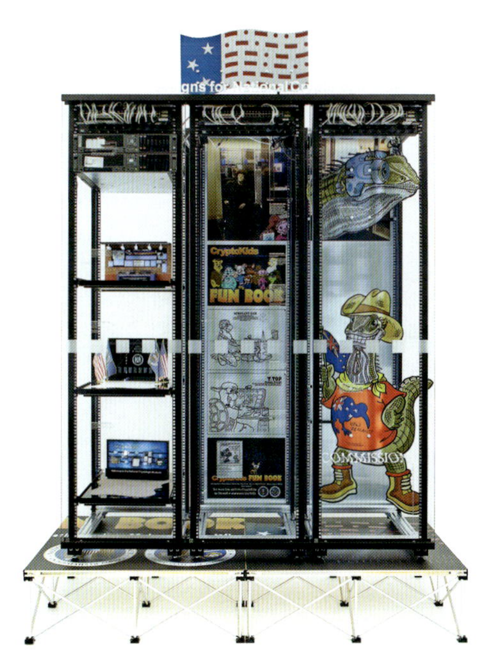

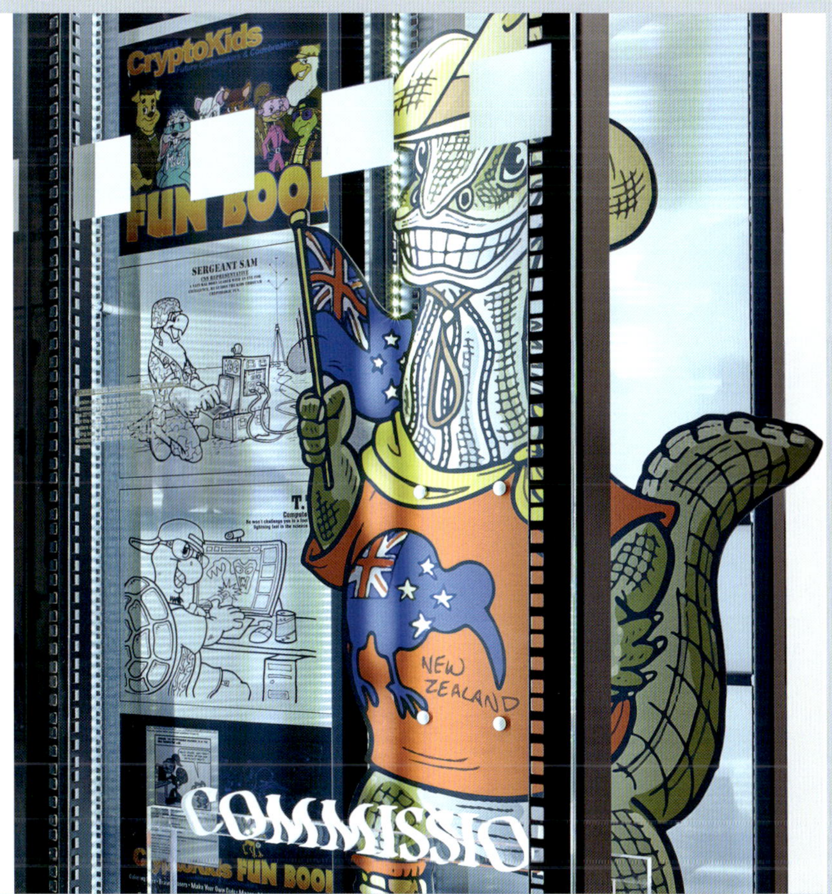

11
12
13
14
15
16
17
18
19
20
21

Here, some of the miniatures are displayed with reproductions of images designed for the NCM in completely customized and enhanced data server racks—with special inset lighting and annotated glass fronts. A digital *Wunderkammer* migrated from low-res JPGs into 3-D models and richly redrawn images. I harvested a lot of images from Darchicourt's online profile and also commissioned new work through his Behance profile. The lizard on the right is based on NSA partner country New Zealand's iconic native tuatara.

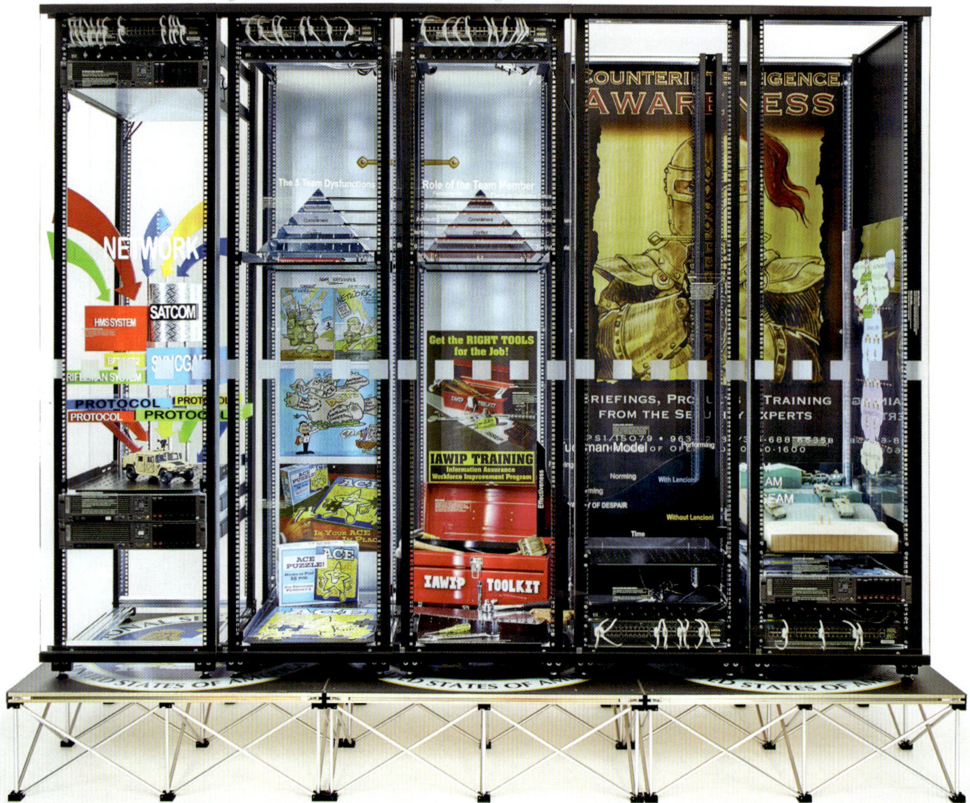

Here, another selection of images from Darchicourt's portfolio was translated into cabinets. These renderings are based on images that were likely all produced for the Defense Intelligence wing of the Agency, where Darchicourt did much of his work.

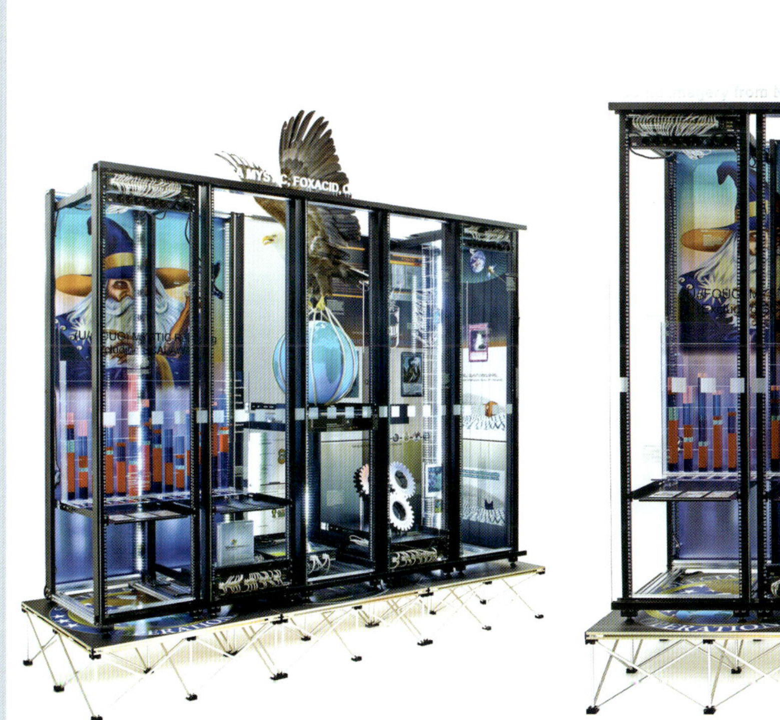
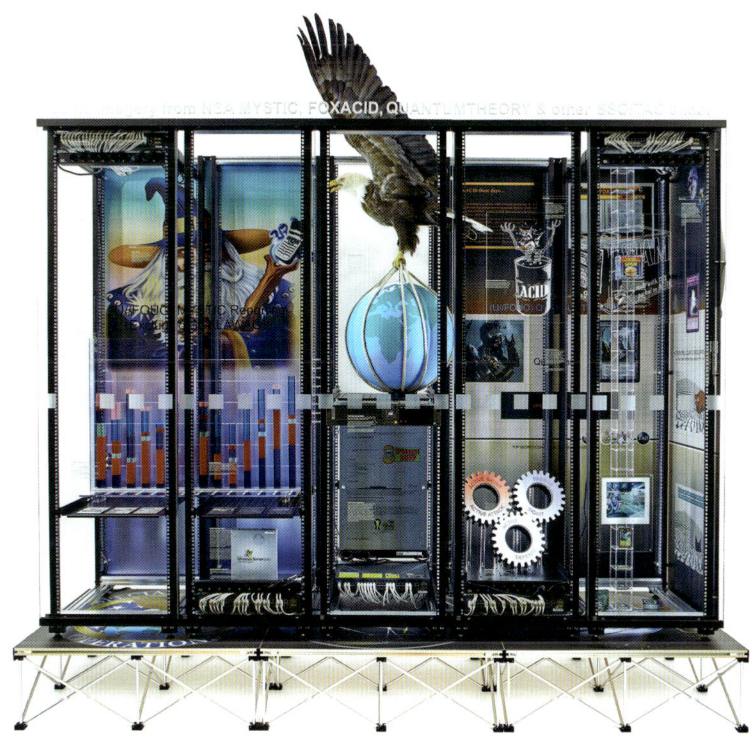

13

14

15

16

17

18

19

20

21

In this cabinet, similar treatment is given to some of the most iconic imagery from the Snowden-leaked documents—authorless images describing some of the most controversial programs outlined in the leaks.

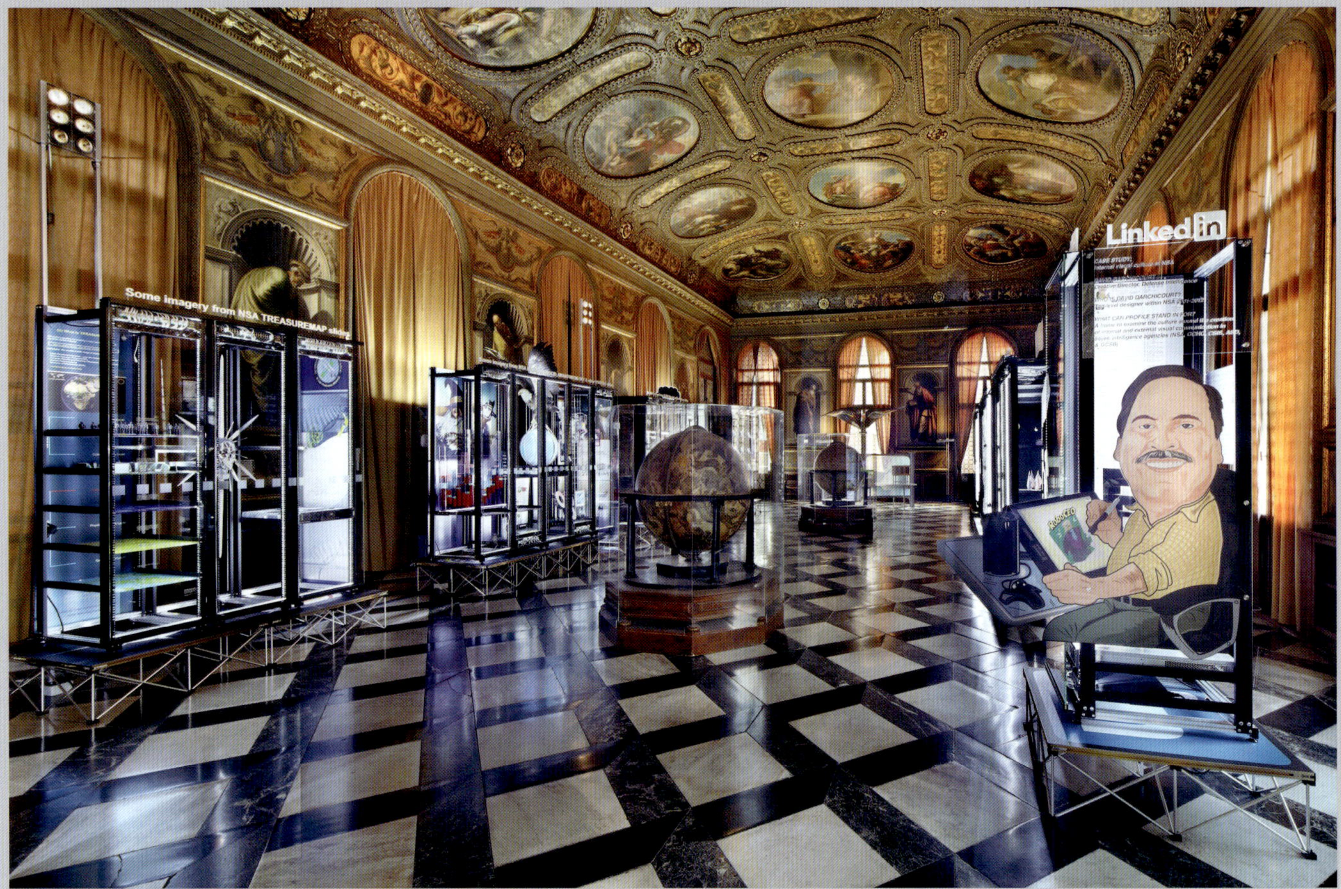

14

My feeling that Darchicourt's work and the work of other illustrators and artists was depicted inside the Agency was underlined in my presentation in Venice's Marciana Library in 2015 (as New Zealand's national pavilion for the Venice Biennale). The vitrines on the right-hand side were those showcasing Darchicourt's work, and the group on the left included anonymous images from various Snowden-leaked slides.

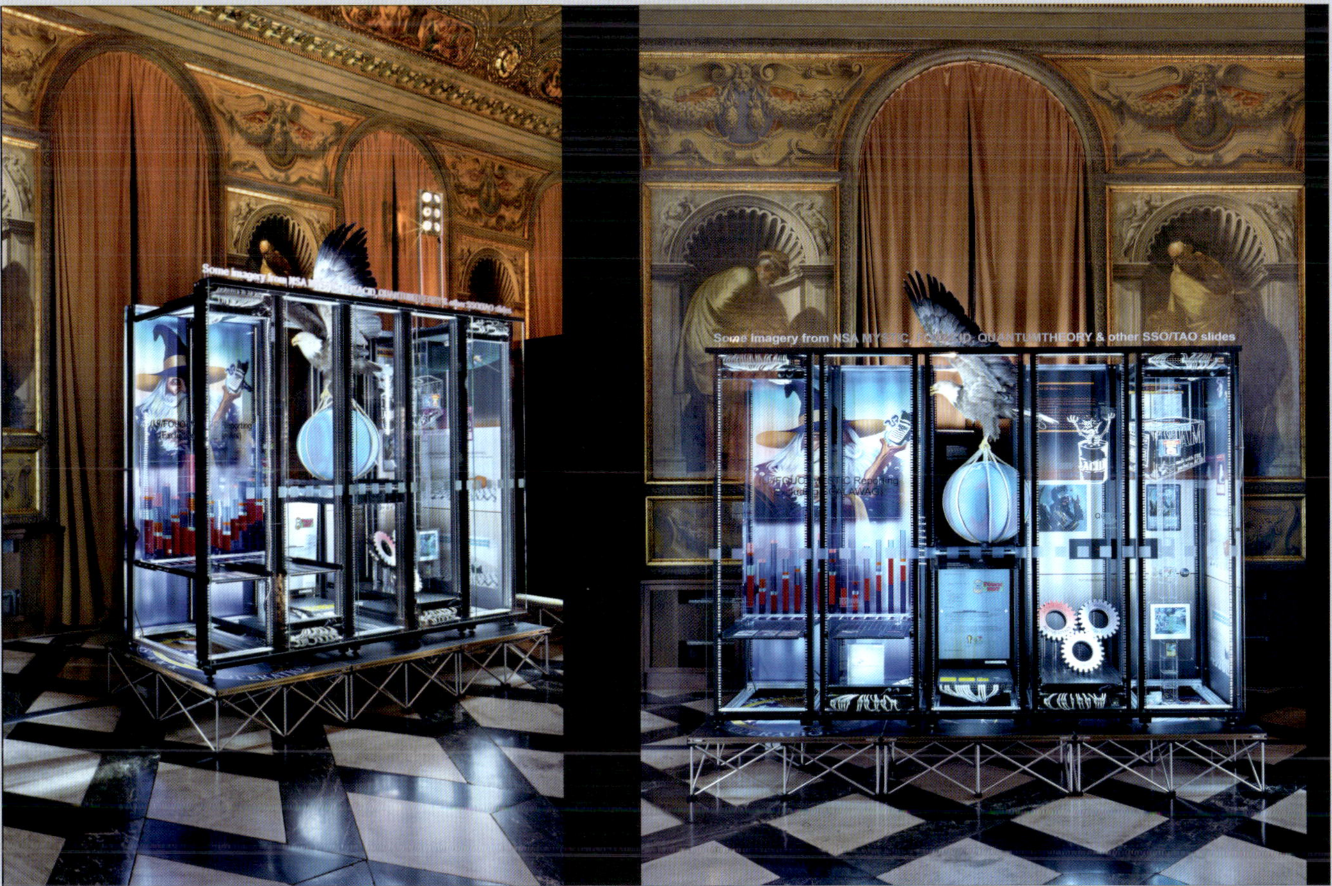

15
16
17
18
19
20
21

The library was designed by fifteenth-century architect Jacopo Sansovino as a giant allegory for the value of knowledge. The walls and ceilings feature paintings illustrating these themes, and the library holds some of the most important maps—geopolitical intelligence visualizations of the Venetian empire—in its grand rooms.

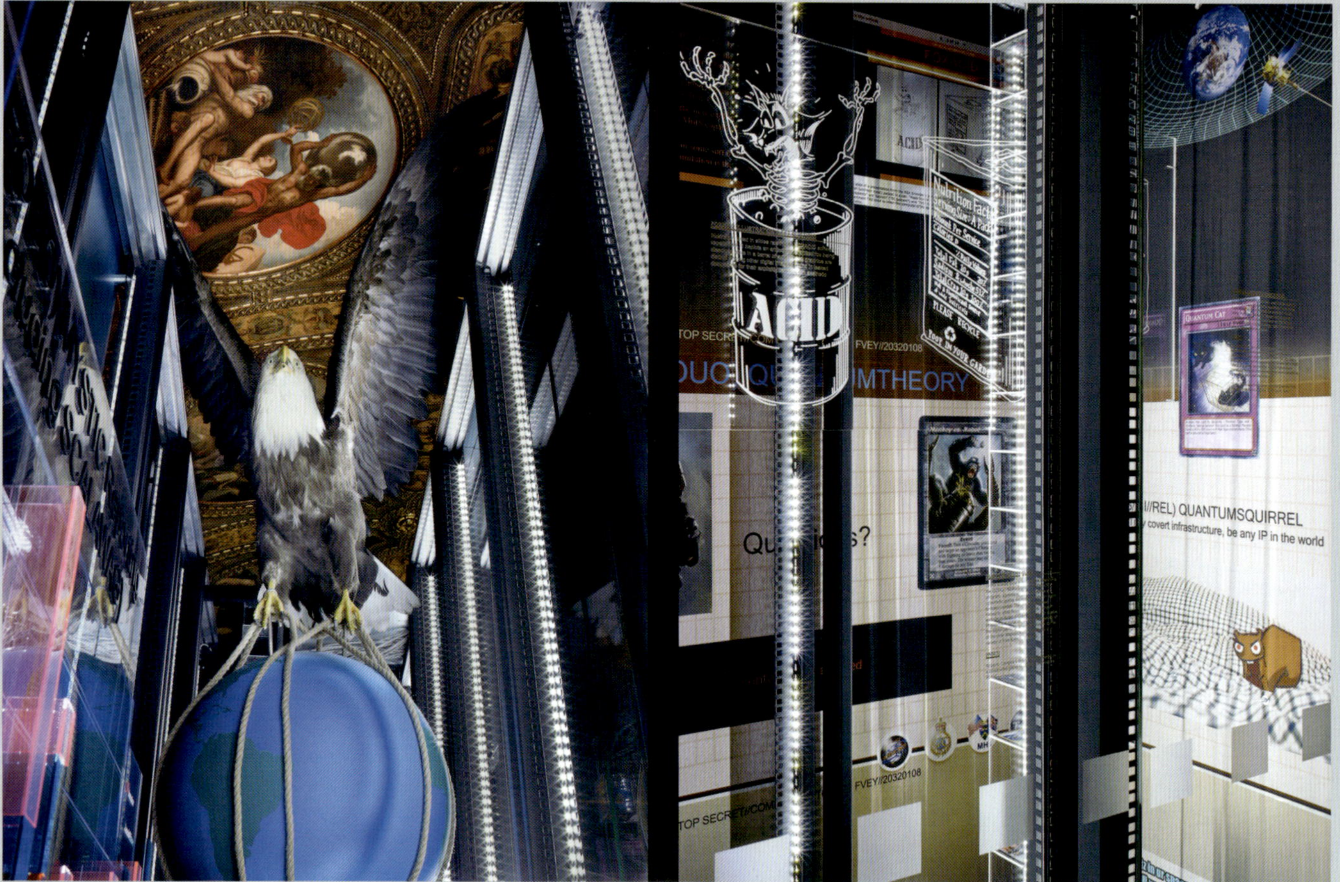

16

17

18

19

20

21

The imagery on globes of fantastic creatures from the Renaissance masters echoed the contemporary images from the NSA, suggesting a powerful historical lineage of ways of describing the importance of information.

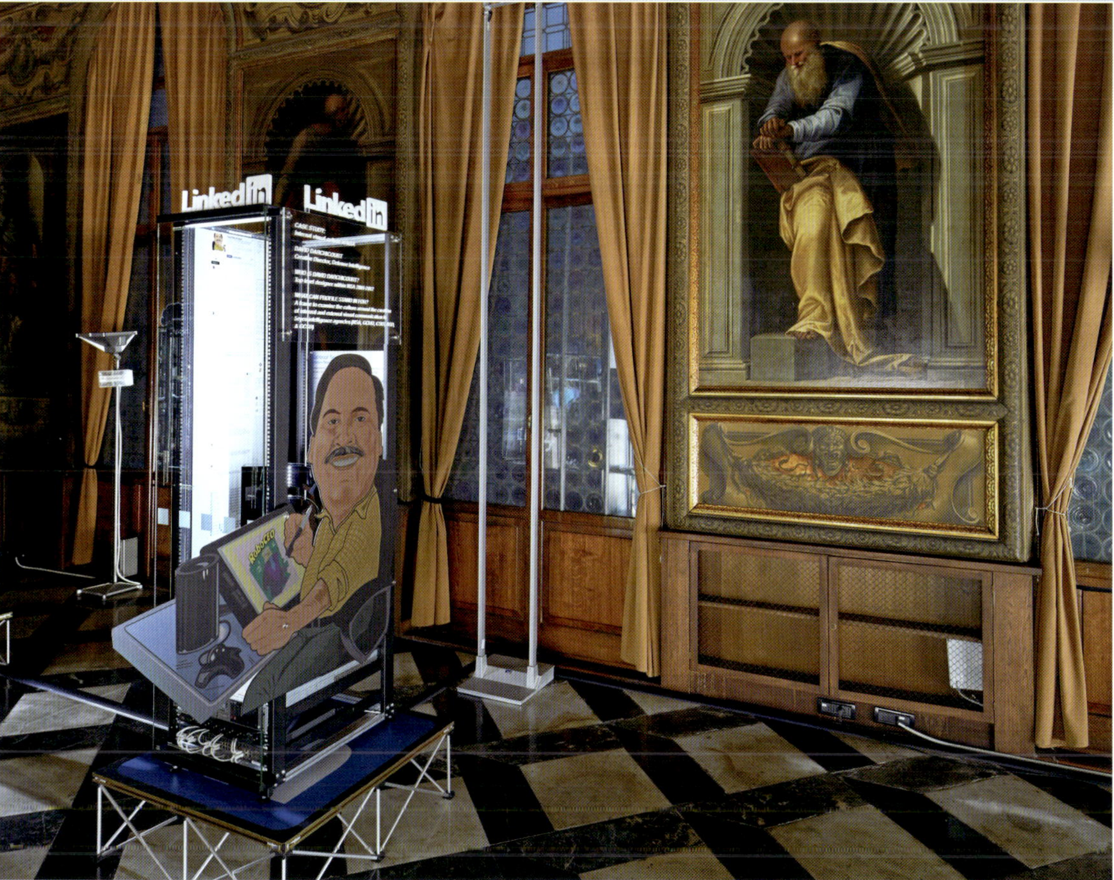

17
18
19
20
21

Strong resonances were suggested in the scale and dialogue between the historical work and the contemporary—giving gravitas to the work of Darchicourt, proposing him as a contemporary aesthetic master of an older genre. The act of employing him and his work for the exhibition was done without his knowledge—so the presentation had a genuine feel of secrecy and illegitimacy to it. The questions raised by Snowden around the appropriateness of the use of data within the NSA were performed with this gesture.

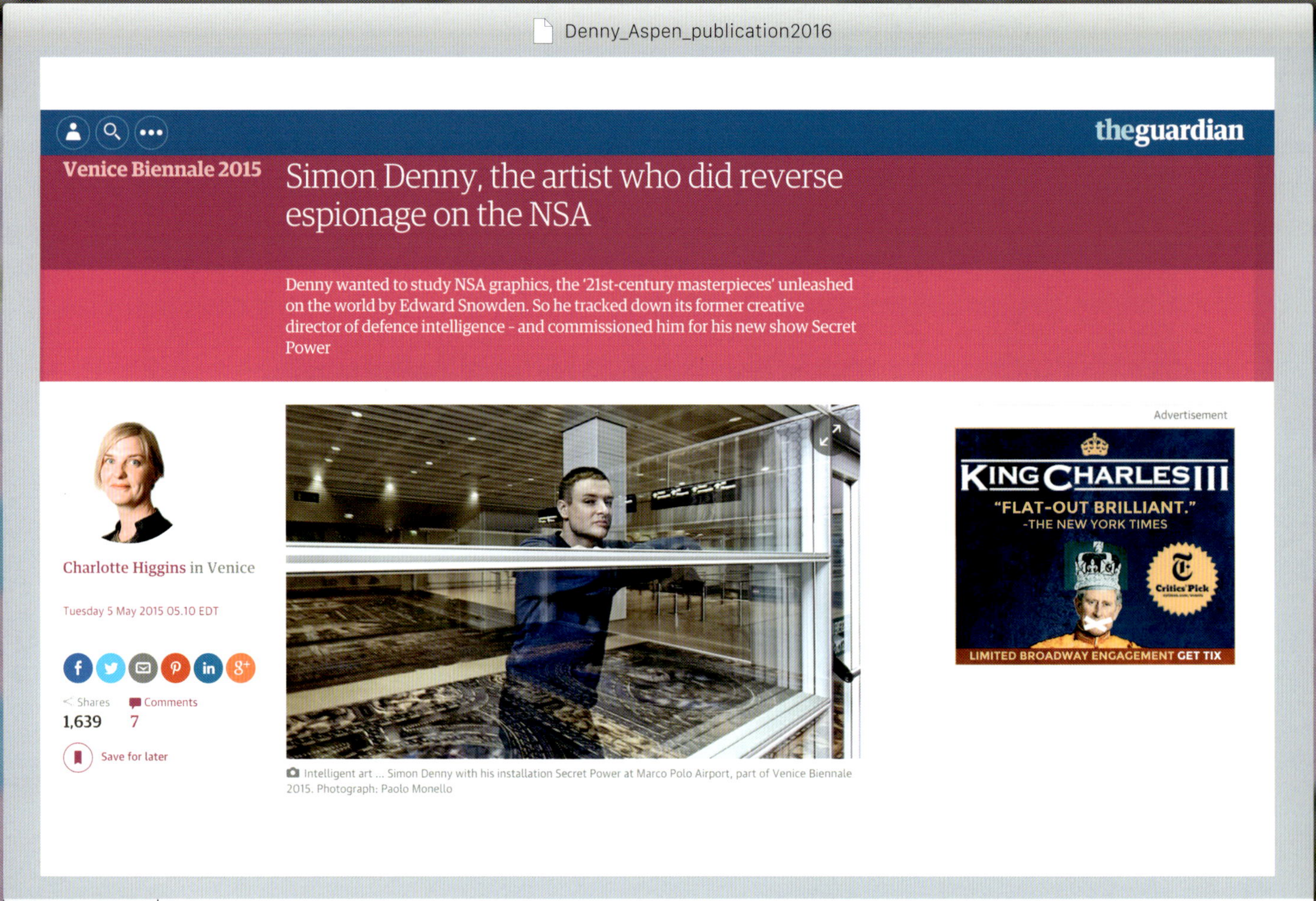

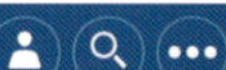

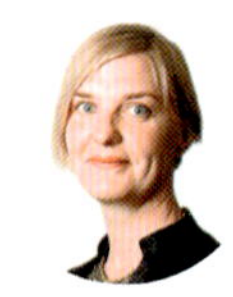

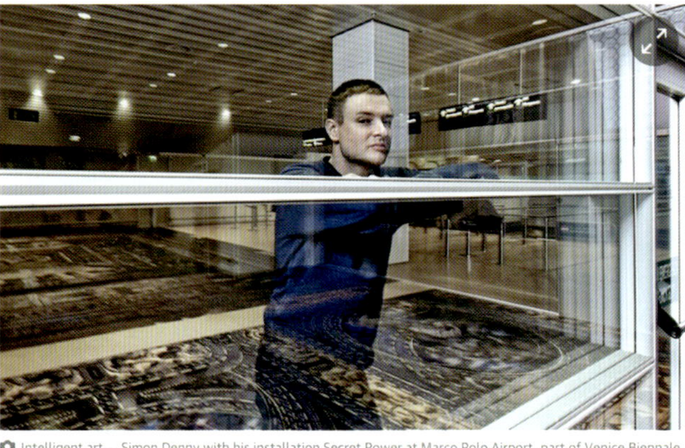

Intelligent art … Simon Denny with his installation Secret Power at Marco Polo Airport, part of Venice Biennale 2015. Photograph: Paolo Monello

The *Guardian*'s lead culture critic, Charlotte Higgins, was given a special preview of the exhibition, and the encounter with Darchicourt's artwork prompted her to contact him for a feature on the exhibition.

He said that he had not personally designed any of the Snowden PowerPoint slides per se, but confirmed to the Guardian that he had, for example, designed the logo used internally at the NSA for the programme Poison Nut - which was 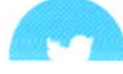 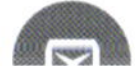 to break through security measures taken by potential targets of surveillance. A document referring to Poison Nut was published by Der Spiegel on 28 December 2014, and its logo - a cartoon squirrel recoiling in horror from a peanut emblazoned with a skull and crossbones - is featured in the show.

When contacted by the Guardian and informed that he was central to Denny's exhibition, Darchicourt confirmed that he had been a graphic designer for the NSA, but added that a non-disclosure agreement prevented him from going into any detail. While surprised, he was sanguine about the use of his work in the exhibition. "I sell my work and I tend not to keep track of it," he said. He added: "I view myself as an Eskimo. They'd do their drawings on pieces of bone, and leave them in their campsites when they left. That's what I do. I was paid very well to do the work [for Venice] and David Bennewith was great to work with. As long as I have credit for my work I am happy."

19 20 21	In her excellent article, Darchicourt is quoted explaining his role in the NSA and reacting to his inclusion in the exhibition. He also revealed himself to be the confirmed author of the "Poisonnut" logo in the Snowden documents.

Describing his role at the NSA, Darchicourt said that his work had been "solving problems visually" and that he was one of two or three people in the organisation's design department skilled in drawing. "My cartooning is something they found useful from time to time - it could be a good communication tool, helping express complex information in a very simple way." "I was particularly involved in working on internal security and security awareness," he said.

20

21

He also identifies the way artists are employed in the Agency and why the cartoon-style visual language is appropriate and useful within the intelligence community—giving real insight into the aesthetic context of the Agency.

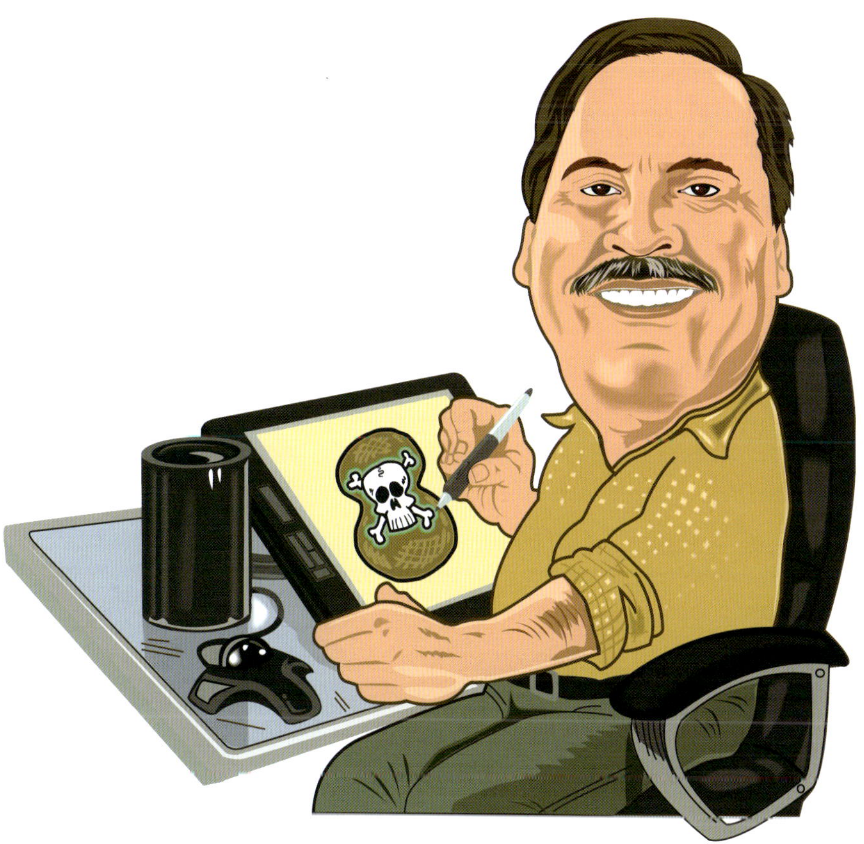

21

Through image-based research, the kind of work done by, until then, anonymous authors was able to be better understood and contextualized. At the time of the exhibition, New Zealand Prime Minister John Key was still denying that the slides leaked by Snowden were real. Attribution through images rendered assertions like these obsolete.

Laura Hoptman

Contentious Curating: Contemporary Painting at MoMA

Recently, I organized a contemporary painting exhibition at the Museum of Modern Art called *The Forever Now: Contemporary Painting in an Atemporal World.* The show featured more than sixty paintings made in the last five years by seventeen artists who, over that period, have been part of a broader discussion about the revival of a neo-modernist abstraction in contemporary art.

MoMA has a history of presenting group exhibitions of contemporary painting. From 1946 until 1963, the legendary MoMA curator Dorothy Miller organized a series of five shows that not only helped cement the careers of artists like Jackson Pollock and Jasper Johns, but also established MoMA as a museum where cutting-edge painting could be seen every few years. Miller's shows were received with intense interest, and also criticism. The *New York Times*, for example, called Miller's *16 Americans*—featuring work by Johns, Ellsworth Kelly, Robert Rauschenberg, and Frank Stella—"unspeakably boring." The regularity with which these exhibitions were presented, though, made contentious discussion an expected, even encouraged element of these shows, and gave them the aspect of propositions rather than pronouncements.

There was a twenty-one-year hiatus between Miller's last contemporary painting exhibition in 1963, and Kynaston McShine's *An International Survey of Recent Painting and Sculpture* in 1984, which also attracted a storm of criticism, ranging from charges of "unforgivable omissions," to "bad hanging." Thirty years later, *The Forever Now* opened in early December 2014, and as expected, attracted most of the same criticisms of Miller's and McShine's exhibitions generations earlier.

Leaving aside the legitimate critiques of all of these shows, there is something about painting itself and the role it has played in art over the past seventy-five years or so that provokes an almost unique level of heated discussion. Painting wasn't always a "problem," but its ever-increasing identity as a commodifiable object, exposed to the vicissitudes of taste and fashion, has made it one. Abstraction has been particularly vulnerable to charges that it is in collusion with the forces of consumption. The use by some critics and art journalists of the term "zombie abstraction" to describe a wide variety of recent abstract paintings is an example of a new kind of pejorative reading that reduces non-figurative canvases to mute objects that signify nothing. It wasn't always this way. Since the beginning of the twentieth century, abstraction has carried the banner of the avant-

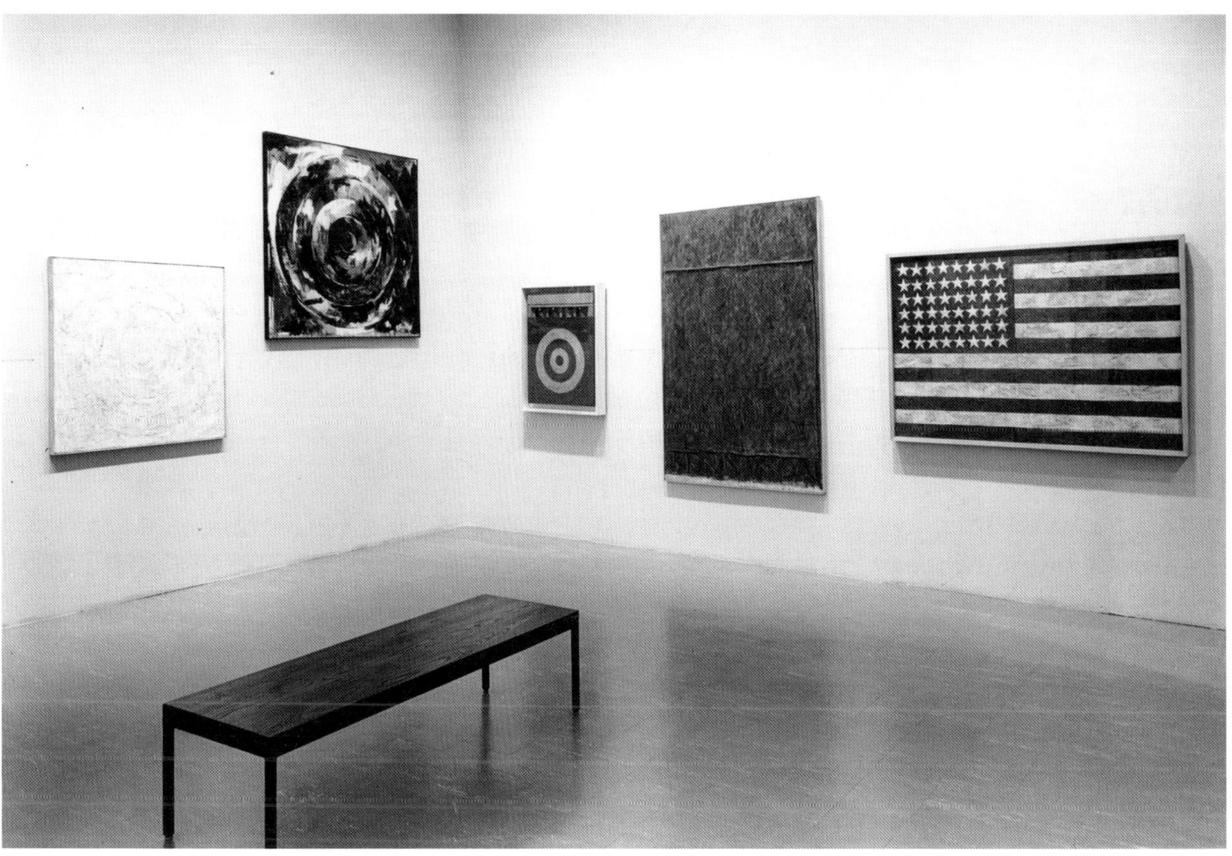

garde, provided a vision for Utopian aesthetics, served as an antidote to the co-optation of art by the forces of totalitarianism, and offered a language with which to articulate the inchoate expressions of the mind and the landscape of a post-nuclear and now digital world.

Today though, with the recycling of a host of abstract languages, in the eyes of many critics, abstraction has lost this connection to the notions of experimentation, risk, and intellectual freedom. It has been demoted as an entire stylistic class to a kind of subject matter. Interestingly, artists have used this to create a mode of abstract painting that is entirely of our moment. This was a central premise of *The Forever Now* and it attracted a chorus of voices questioning the exhibition's relationship to the hot market in contemporary painting.

Abstract painting has been rendered suspect in today's market-driven contemporary art ecosystem, but so is an exhibition platform like MoMA, a museum that houses the greatest collection of European and American modern art in the world. Any time MoMA exhibits very new art, its canonical works—from Vincent van Gogh's *The Starry Night* (1889) to

Installation view: *Sixteen Americans*, December 16, 1959– February 17, 1960. The Museum of Modern Art, New York. Gelatin-silver print, 7 1/4 x 9 1/2 in (18.4 x 24.1 cm). Photographic Archive. The Museum of Modern Art Archives, New York. Photo: Rudy Burckhardt

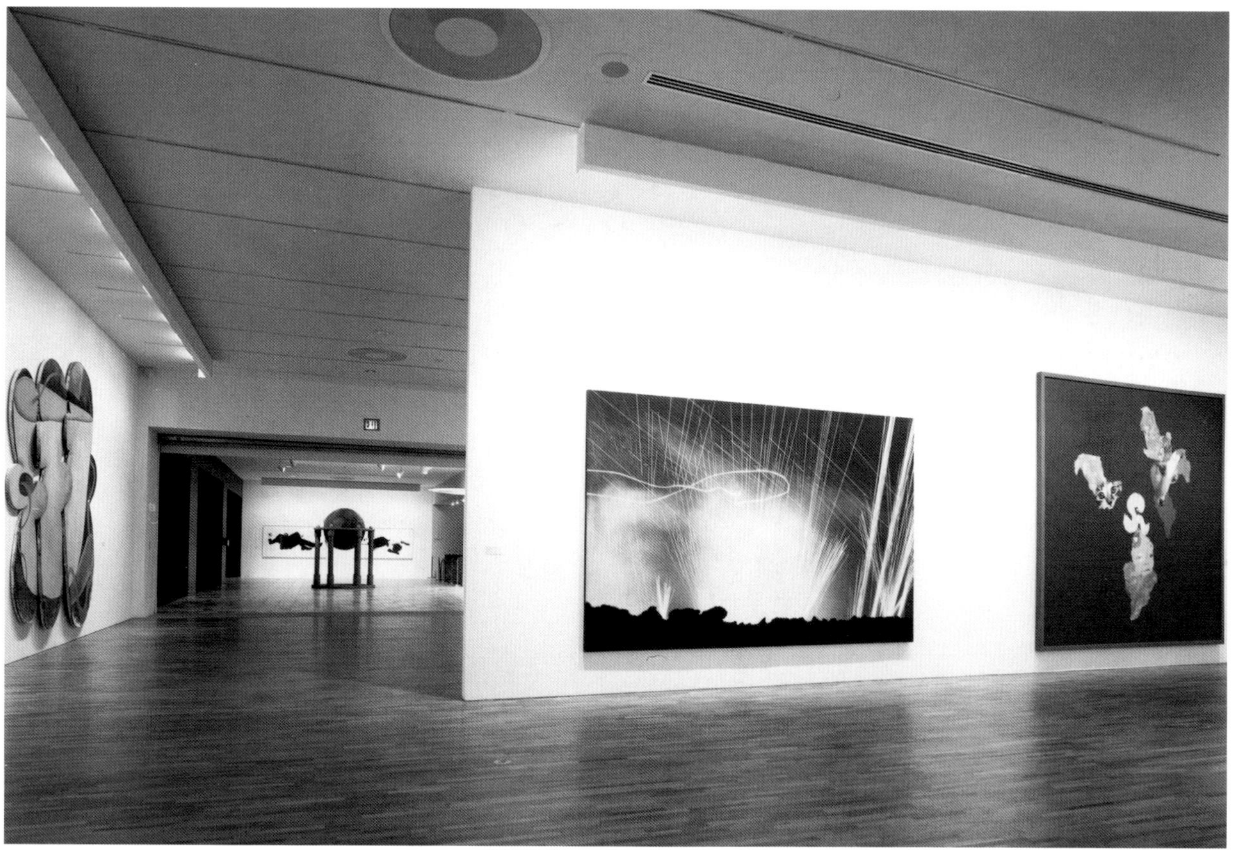

Barnett Newman's *Vir Heroicus Sublimis* (1950–51)—create the context. As a result, many see a show of contemporary art in a traditional medium like painting as a display of presumptive masterpieces. The MoMA context confers gravitas, but it also implies importance, quality, even "value" in the economic sense. This creates a curatorial conundrum; if a contemporary exhibition at MoMA features lesser-known artists, it runs the risk of canonizing them, but more perilously, creating economic value. If we exhibit art to which value has already been conferred, the museum might be seen as shoring up the marketplace. In any scenario, a show of new painting can be interpreted as inherently problematic—some say, collusive—with the roaring, speculative contemporary art market.

In New York, with its vast community of commercial art galleries, there has been much discussion among museum curators about how a public can differentiate between an exhibition at an enormous commercial gallery and one at an art museum. The most obvious difference lies in the fact that though museums might collect contemporary art, they do not sell it.

Installation view: *International Survey of Recent Painting and Sculpture*, May 17, 1984–August 19, 1984. The Museum of Modern Art, New York. Gelatin-silver print, 7 x 9 in (17.8 x 22.9 cm). Photographic Archive. The Museum of Modern Art Archives, New York. © The Museum of Modern Art, New York. Photo: Katherine Keller

In fact, most museums (MoMA included) prohibit the sale of work in the collection by living artists. In contradistinction to a gallery show, the motivation of a museum exhibition is not to enhance value, but to argue for *worthiness*, a distinction that includes historic importance and contemporary relevance, in addition to aesthetic interest. While gallery exhibitions must necessarily come and go with swiftness, their rhythm keyed to the influx and distribution of goods, museum exhibitions, and the scholarly materials that accompany them, are less ephemeral. Their goal is to present (or perhaps start) an argument that will begin a discussion that one hopes will live on in the cultural discourse.

It is a point of pride for me to emphasize that the most contentious element of MoMA's most recent contemporary painting exhibition was not the choice of artists, nor the hanging of the show, but its premise. *The Forever Now* was a contemporary painting show, but it was also an argument that a broader cultural phenomenon—what the futurologist and science-fiction author William Gibson called "atemporality"—is evident in painting today. Atemporality describes a state of contemporary culture in which, courtesy of the internet, styles from all eras exist at once, and no one style can claim to represent our moment. Taking advantage of this avalanche of information, artists working atemporally create works of art that are a rich mix of borrowings, allusions, and reinterpretations from all over the art historical timeline, but especially from the past century. They reanimate, reenact, or sample from the history of art without a trace of parody or nostalgia. They challenge past styles to be relevant again in our "endless digital Now,"[1] as Gibson has described our time.

Artists have always looked to art history for inspiration, but the hugely expanded catalogue of visual information that is available digitally has radically altered their relationship to history. It is no longer seen as a beginning-to-end progression from one innovation to another, but as a broad, horizontal field that invites exploration from any point. This new use and assimilation of dizzying varieties of sources has a pseudomorphic relationship to appropriation in the 1980s sense of the word, the weapon of choice for postmodern critique of originality, the object, and the institution. However, this new era of super-charged art historicism is neither critical nor ironic; it's not even nostalgic. It is closest to a connoisseurship of boundless information, a picking and choosing of elements of the past as a tool, as a subject, or both.

For some cultural critics, the rise of atemporality is not a happy turn of events. Absence of stylistic markers can indicate the demise of a common culture, a deeply troubling development, which at best, indicates cultural stasis, and at worst, cultural surrender. Simon Reynolds, a music critic who coined the term "retromania" to describe the recent phenomenon of reanimation and sampling of musical genres of the past fifty years, sees

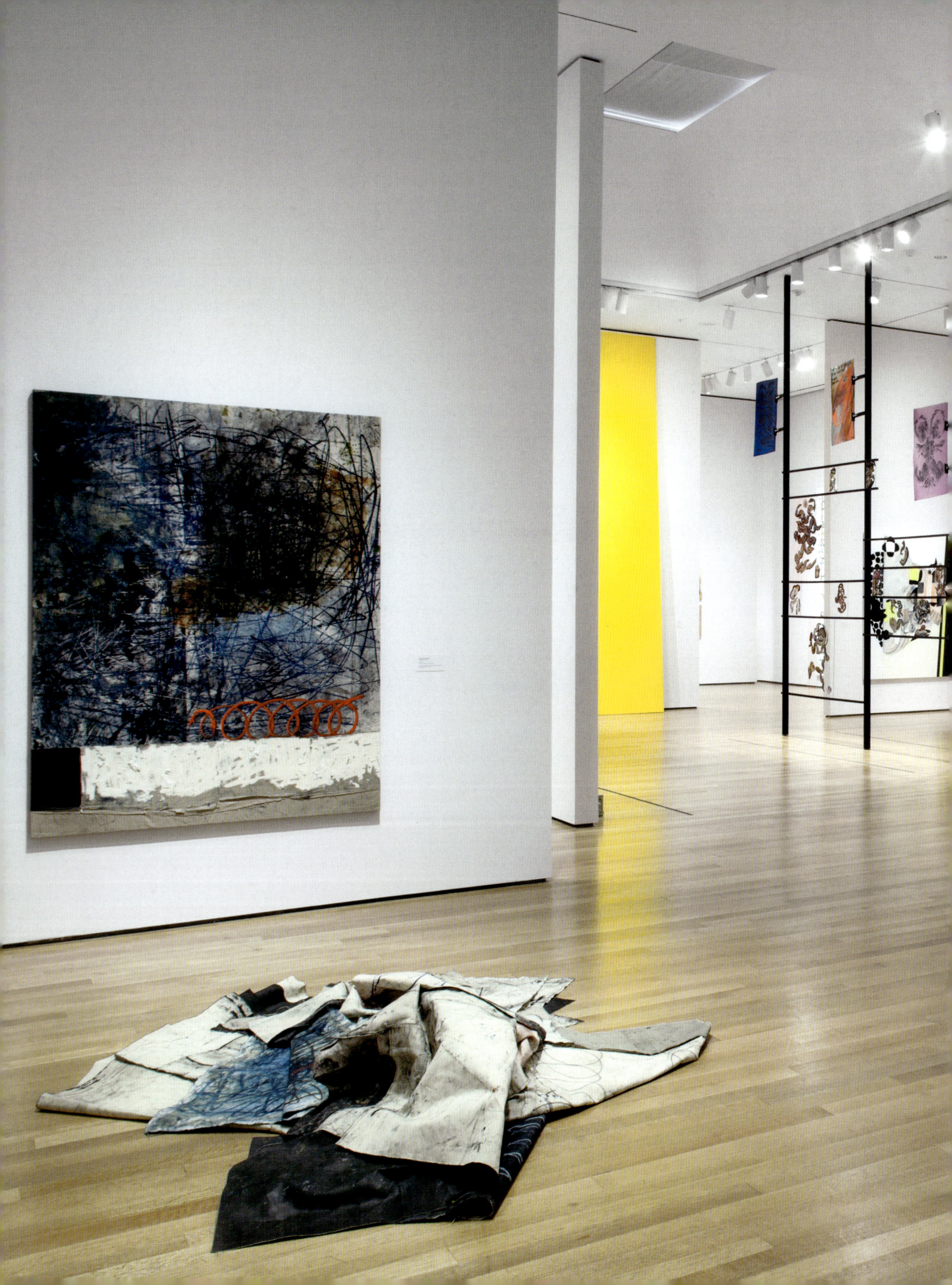

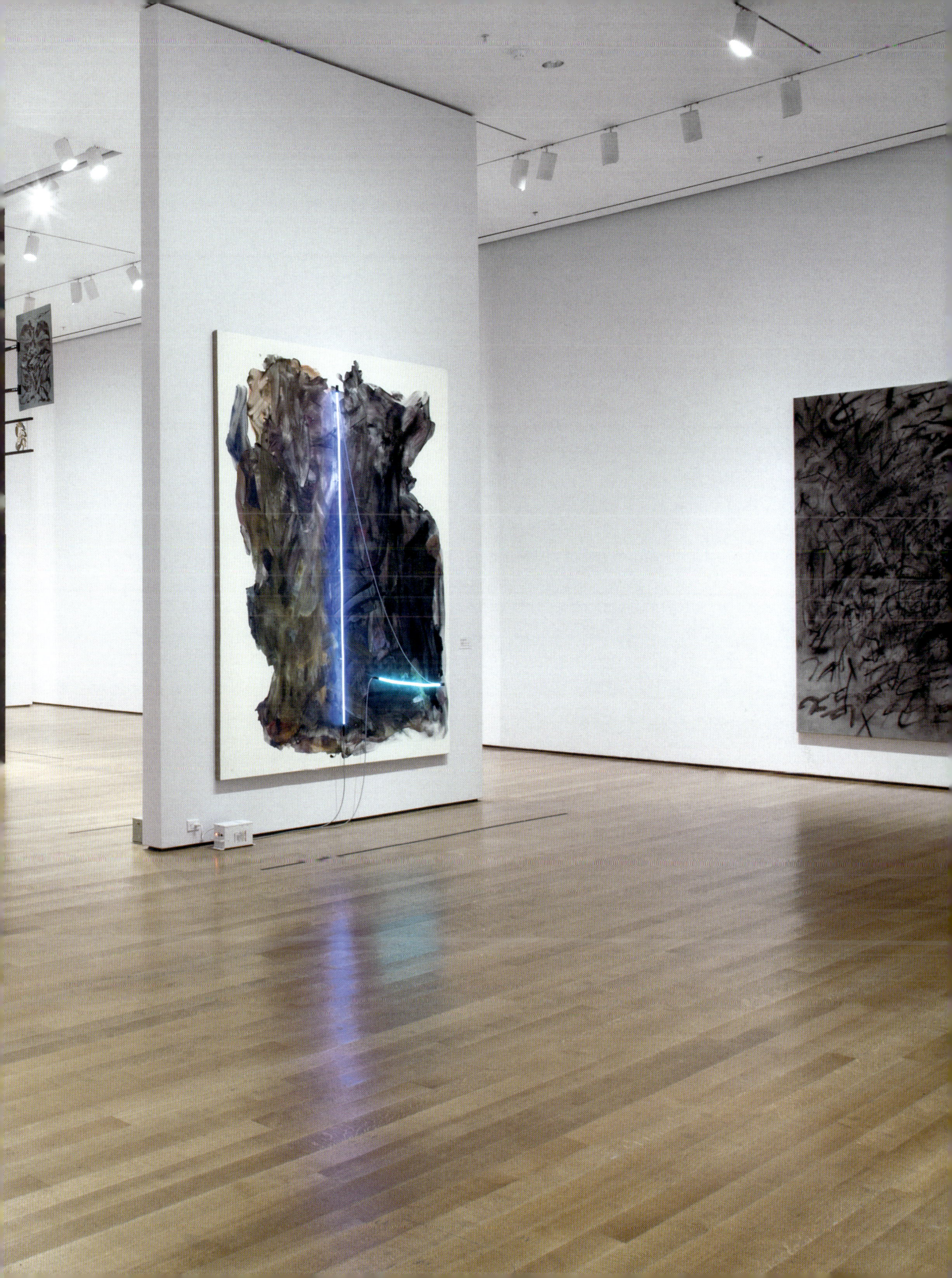

the erosion of era-defining genres as an intellectual dead end.[2] "We're quite deep into a phase of anything-goes, guiltless appropriation, a free-for-all of asset-stripping that ranges all over the globe and all across the span of human history," he wrote in his 2011 book *Retromania*. "This leads to the paradoxical combination of speed and standstill."[3] These observations, echoed by literary, fashion, and lately, art pundits, reveal an acute nostalgia for a time when things were new, and a deep mourning for the propulsive shot of energy that attended an act of what could be interpreted as cultural progress. Many critics of *The Forever Now* echoed Reynolds's fears, criticizing the paintings in the exhibition as unoriginal pastiches. Others denied the notion of atemporality altogether, claiming that the reanimation of past styles in contemporary painting was itself an updated manifestation of 1980s appropriation.

Atemporality might make people—and art critics, in particular— uncomfortable because it is a different way of looking at history; one that refutes the idea of progress. By pointing out that some artists decide not to put any new information into our cultural system, atemporality posits not only a non-teleological cultural landscape, but a non-growth one as well. Atemporality might be unsettling because, at its base, it is a strategy of resistance, a way of "opting out of the industrialization of novelty"[4] (in William Gibson's terms) and the syndrome of growth and expansion at any cost. In a way, abstaining from the creation of new aesthetic forms means gaining new ways of understanding the use of form in light of digital technology and the swift circulation of knowledge. In addition, the promiscuous mixing of styles might have the positive outcome of providing a mechanism to overcome onerous traditions and even aversion to cultural difference.

The implications of this might be scary, but they are also exhilarating. For one, the criteria for judging contemporary art changes. It no longer has to be based on the idea of "new form," but the idea of "relevant form." Originality then, doesn't have to be predicated on putting something new into the system, but rather, something we can use. Secondly, atemporality lays waste to the idea that there is a single cultural narrative—or even a dominant "taste" or overarching trend. Atemporality creates the possibility of many stories happening simultaneously, which we can all agree is evident in our visual culture today. Finally, there can be a change of heroes and heroines of contemporary culture, torpedoing for good the problematic connection between artistic form and real politics that was born in the early twentieth century. This is a connection that still hangs on the privileging of the non-object (as progressive) over the object, like an abstract painting—vulnerable to interpretation as a mere auratic ornament, and as such, reactionary and complicit with the commodification of culture.

PREVIOUS: Installation view: *The Forever Now: Contemporary Painting in an Atemporal World*, December 14, 2014–April 5, 2015. The Museum of Modern Art, New York. © The Museum of Modern Art, New York. Photo: John Wronn

It might not be apparent yet, but there is an ethics to making art in an atemporal way. What we lose in scuttling the ideal of progress, we recuperate in the invigorating thought of the infinite possibilities of re-evaluation, remixing, and retrofitting. The poly-chronological crazy quilts of assembled cultural data suggest that artists who boldly pick from their precursors have the potential to scramble our historical hierarchies, banish polarities such as "progressive" or "reactionary," and frustrate rigid regimes of taste. Counter to the fear of chronological malaise that atemporal tendencies in culture strike in the hearts of some, this is a hopeful, even invigorating quest, one that encourages the continued exploration of a vast, synchronic landscape of information peculiar to our century, in search of a broader, bolder notion of what painting and indeed what culture can be. This was the goal of *The Forever Now*, which I believe it had in common with the contemporary painting exhibitions at MoMA over the last sixty years. And if it started a critical conversation, albeit a heated one that continues to rage, it should be remembered as another addition to that long-running series.

[1] William Gibson, talk at Book Expo America, 2010, cited in Simon Reynolds, *Retromania: Pop Culture's Addiction to its Own Past* (New York: Faber and Faber, 2011), 397.
[2] Simon Reynolds, "The Songs of Now Sound a Lot Like Then," *New York Times*, July 17, 2011, AR14.
[3] Reynolds, *Retromania*, 426–27.
[4] William Gibson, *Zero History* (New York: Penguin, 2010), 116.

Betty Woodman

in conversation with Heidi Zuckerman

In the following interview between Betty Woodman and Heidi Zuckerman, which took place in February 2016, the artist discusses the development of her practice as well as her installation The Aspen Garden Room *(1984).*

Heidi Zuckerman I wanted to talk a little bit about your career in a broader way, and also specifically about your time in Colorado as well as your 1984 exhibition at the Aspen Art Museum, which was just recently restaged in London at Frieze. Maybe you could start off by talking about how you found yourself in Colorado and teaching here originally?

Betty Woodman When my husband George graduated from Harvard in 1954, he was accepted into the University of New Mexico for a master's degree in painting, so we moved to Albuquerque. Then he got a job at the University of Colorado, teaching Theory of Art and Art Criticism and Painting, so we moved there in 1956. Twenty years later, I started teaching there.

HZ What were you doing for those twenty years?

BW I was in my studio making work, first in Albuquerque and then in Colorado. At that point in my life, I was a potter and making what was essentially functional work. When I began teaching, it was for the City of Boulder Recreational Department, which had started a pottery program. Initially, there were seven students once a week; by the time I finished, there were four hundred students every eight weeks. It became a large, successful program that served a real function in the city of Boulder in the fifties, sixties, and seventies. I was interested in teaching at the university, but there weren't any jobs. It was a one-person department with Tom Potter. It wasn't until they finally decided to expand the department that I applied and started working there.

HZ You made reference to the fact that the ceramic work you were making at the time was functional. Can you talk about how you define your practice and how you would categorize the evolution of your work?

BW When I finished school in 1949, I wanted to make functional objects that would serve society—I felt that having beautiful things to use was an important contribution to the world. My work evolved, and continues to evolve, but not in a very self-conscious way. The pieces became less committed to function—though function is always there as a subject matter—and they span a wider stage now.

I also went to Italy in 1951 and became aware of a whole Mediterranean influence on clay. It expanded my awareness of the history of ceramics and connected my own work to a certain past, be it of painting, clay, or sculpture. What an amazing rich history of ceramics there is. What one can do with clay is never-ending.

I started working at a low temperature and was very interested in the surface and painting, and the marriage of painting and form—which is, as far as I'm concerned, what ceramics is all about. I was dealing with traditional forms, but then started playing with their scales and building up to architectural pieces like *The Aspen Garden Room* (1984). The history of clay is involved with architecture—and there is always a connection to previous works of art in my pieces, objects made with the same materials that I'm using.

Though it was originally my goal to be a potter—and the work I did grew out of that—it's not what I'm doing today and it's not what the work is about (if we need some cups, however, I'll sit down and make some). At a certain point, I started seeing what I was creating as painting or sculpture, and not as pottery. When I made *The Aspen Garden Room*, it wasn't just about architecture, it was also about combining different materials—clay as well as fabrics.

I'm still working with collage fabrics today. There are certain things that are attractive and keep pulling me in—I go back over the same territory, but I'm really doing very different things each time.

HZ   How did the Aspen show in 1984 come about?

BW   That's an interesting question because I just don't remember. I'm sure it was through Sissy Thomas who was the Director at Ronald Greenberg's gallery. I'm sure she asked if I would like to do a show.

HZ   Do you remember coming for a site visit? Did you make the work in response to the specific architecture of the space?

BW   I had a floor plan and knew what the size limitations were, but I didn't make the work in response to the space's specific architecture— the piece evolved over a period of time.

In 1979, Kippy Stroud invited me to make a project at the Fabric Workshop in Philadelphia. I made three silkscreens on a canvas-like material and then cut them up and pasted them together to make three different doorways and doorframes. My interest in frames goes back to when I received a Fulbright to go to Florence in 1965, and George and I

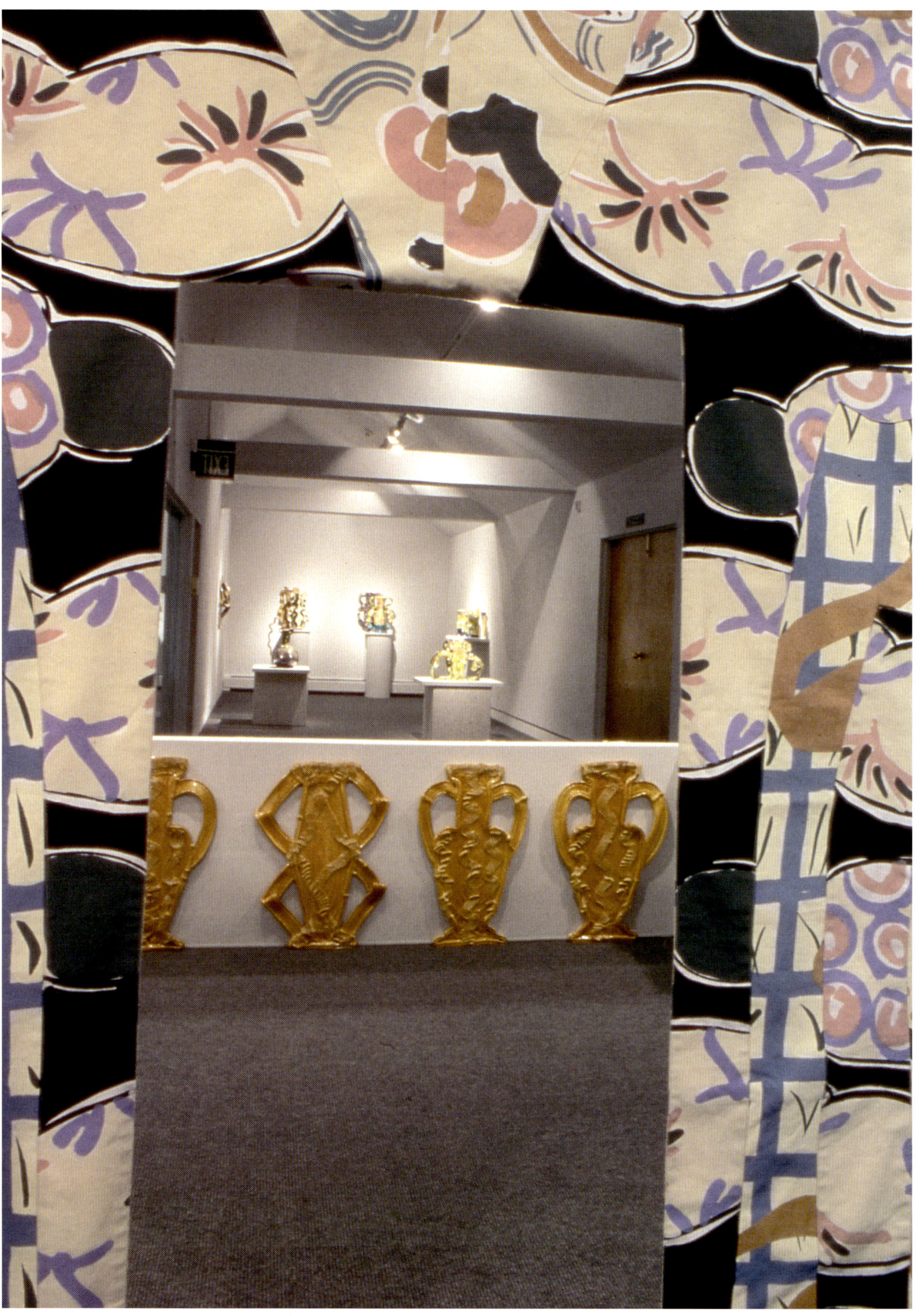

spent the year there. I made a lot of pieces in Italy based on Renaissance architecture and on the details of Florence's windows. A window is just a rectangle, but then with a frame, it changes the way you see it. It's something that I've been interested in for a long time.

The first architectural piece I made, *A Cloistered Arbor Room* (1981), was in a show in Bennington College's gallery. They built a room for me and I made a fabric doorway for it. The interior had tiles and flat columns around the space. Following this, I was asked to do the show at the Aspen Art Museum. I took the doorway and tiles from *A Cloistered Arbor Room* and elaborated on them in a different way. The room that you entered disappeared and became like a garden wall.

HZ It's nice to have a reference to Kippy Stroud and the Fabric Workshop.

BW Exactly. The last conversation I had with Kippy was about putting the Aspen piece up in London and what I should do when I got the fabric doorway—how I should have it cleaned. Anyway, after she passed away, it was very touching for me to be able to install the piece in London.

HZ The chairs and tables in the piece at Frieze weren't included in the original presentation. Where did they come from?

BW No, not at all. That was Jeanne Greenberg-Rohatyn adding those to the booth. They were by Diego Giacometti.

HZ Were the pieces that sit on the tables included in the Aspen show?

BW No, the Aspen show wasn't really like the London presentation. I didn't try to re-create the piece, we just tried to adapt it to the space of the booth. It's actually a free-standing sculpture, but it has four walls and you can walk around the outside of it.

HZ Did you include real plants in the original piece?

BW Yes, the geraniums inside were real.

HZ That's interesting. Then the forms that surround the geraniums really take the shape of absent furniture.

BW They do. The forms are very much based on Italian windows—they play on the window box. I actually did a whole series of window pieces in Italy that I showed at Freedman Gallery in Pennsylvania.

HZ The columns around the back of the space don't look like fragments, they look like they were complete. Was the intention to have shorter columns?

BW Right, like you might have a series of posts around a garden. They weren't supposed to be fragments— they were completed.

Installation view: Betty Woodman, *The Aspen Garden Room*, March 24–June 24, 1984. Aspen Art Museum

HZ   There are interesting elements in the tiling on the interior that reference a grid and then there are multiple organic references, particularly the green columns along the front, as well as the fabric. Were you playing with the idea of mixing geometric and organic?

BW   I think I was, absolutely. The tall green columns with capitals on top of them also reference Greek columns.

HZ   Were there intentional Asian references in the fabric patterns?

BW   I suppose there were with the Japanese screen-painting. The fabrics were really influenced by the ceramics. I was making platters with a similar brushstroke—one platter was inspired by an Islamic bowl at the Metropolitan Museum.

I'm interested in the functional object and how it sits within a discourse of art. My work is never totally clear in terms of the references, because you can read so many different things into it. And there tends to be a kind of richness, so as you stay with the piece, it changes. None of this is immediately obvious, but usually there are a lot of hints of references. I like to have multiple parts in front of me and then figure out how they go together.

Betty Woodman in *The Aspen Garden Room*, March 24—June 24, 1984. Aspen Art Museum

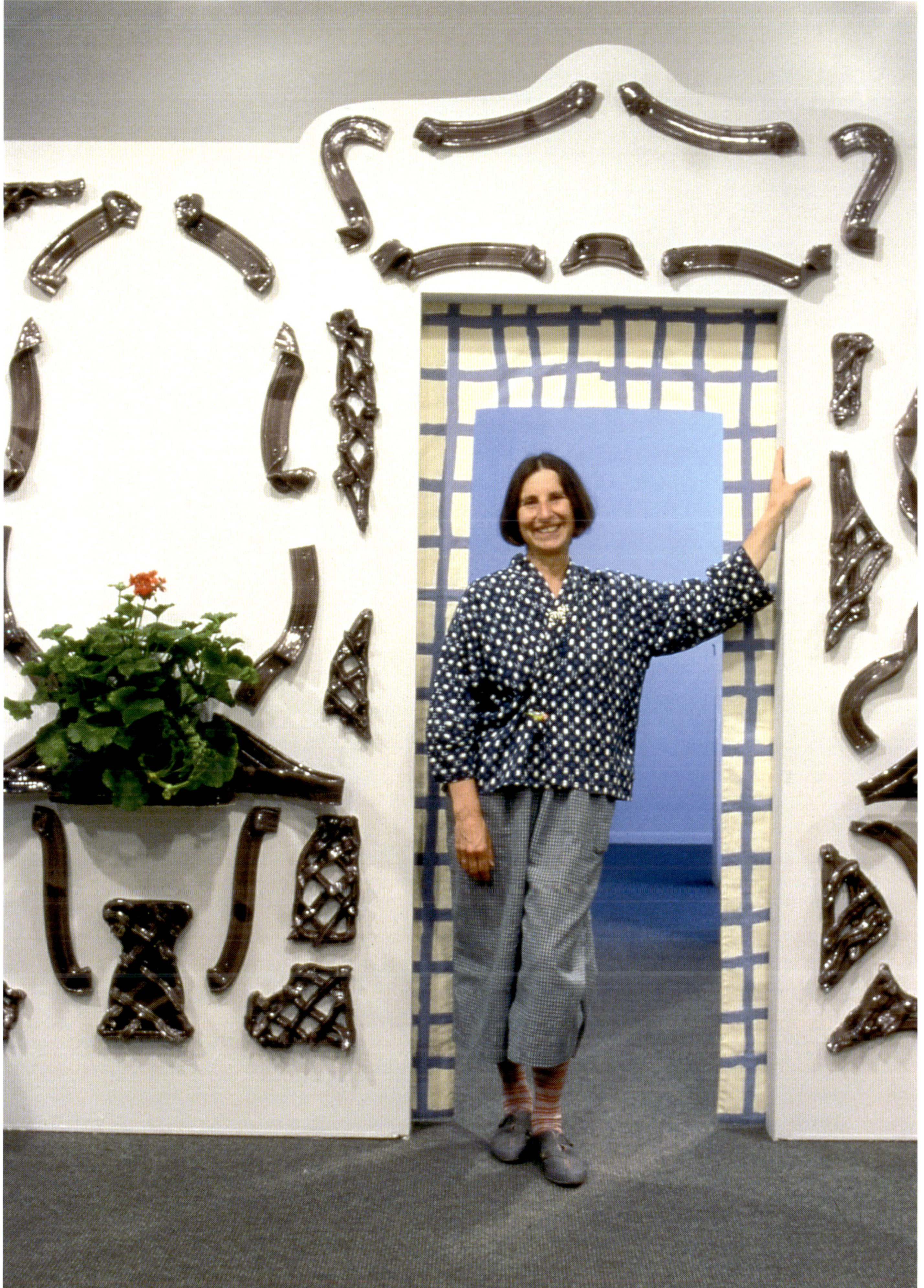

Rodney Graham

Fig. 0

Figure 1 shows the 1971 advertisement for van Laack shirts, which appeared in the German magazine *Der Spiegel* in 1971 and featured artist Marcel Broodthaers as a model. I assume he did it for money. He always needed it. The owners of the company were collectors and later Broodthaers gave them a folded white shirt with a dedication on the cuff (Fig. 2), perhaps as a New Year's gift.

The caption below the van Laack photograph reads:

> The Director of the Musée d'Art Moderne, Département
> des Aigles [Marcel Broodthaers], refused to wear the
> van Laack monocle.

I can find no further reference to the van Laack monocle, but one thinks immediately of the Hathaway man's eye patch (Fig. 3). I do anyway. Perhaps the photographer or stylist wanted to evoke the famous American ad campaign that turned a small, local Maine shirtmaker into the number one producer of dress shirts in the world, but Broodthaers thought better of it. He was right. It would have been too much. The cigar is enough.

I must have known of this image of Broodthaers in 1992 when, in my belatedness, I staged my own modest intervention into the fashion world, collaborating with the Belgian designer Ann Demeulemeester on a white shirt (Fig. 4)—a shirt I never modeled, though Ann made it in my size. However, I certainly did know of the importance of the poet Stéphane Mallarmé for Broodthaers when we titled the work *White Shirt (for Mallarmé)*.

I had the privilege of working on the project with my great friend Yves Gevaert, who knew Broodthaers well, having curated two exhibitions of the artist's work at the Palais de Beaux-Arts in Brussels and collaborated on several publications with him, including *Pauvre Belgique*. He spoke often of Broodthaers and I believe it was Yves who showed me a copy of Broodthaers's version of Mallarmé's *Un Coup de Dés Jamais N'Abolira Le Hasard* (Fig. 5).

We know that, as a teenager, Broodthaers received a copy of *Un Coup de Dés* from René Magritte, for whom Mallarmé was also important. Though I find no reference in Broodthaers's work to an early 1864 prose poem by Mallarmé called *The Demon Of Analogy*, this does not mean he did not know it. It was this poem that I had printed on the kind of card stock around which shirts are folded, at least in North America, when they return from the dry cleaners. Some of the words of the poem ("The Penultimate is dead") are detached from the rest of the text and printed on transparent tissue, similarly used by dry cleaners, which is superimposed on the card. I know where this came from: Broodthaers's edition of *Un Coup de Dés* is printed on the same kind of transparent "cigarette paper."

In Mallarmé's poem, the poet leaves his apartment and finds himself muttering an absurd phrase under his breath: "La Pénultième est morte." The descending "nul" sound in "Pénultième" is accompanied, in a kind of synesthesia, by the description of a bird's wing drawn bowlike in a downward, caressing movement across the strings of an instrument.

He tries to interpret it, but it defies analysis. "Pénultième," however, reminds him of his daily struggle, what the poet does for money—teaching English. He convinces himself that the word "pénultième" means the second-to-last syllable of a word, sometimes stressed in English, never in French.

The words keep rhythmically tumbling around in his head, detaching themselves even further from meaning, approaching pure music as he walks. He finds himself on a street of antiquarian dealers. Pausing in front of a lute-maker's shop, in the window's reflection, he sees himself making a downward-strumming gesture mingled with objects within the store—a tableau of bird wings, palm fronds, and stringed instruments.

Window shopping, window dressing. If this poem precedes Mallarmé's involvement in the fashion industry by a decade—when he edited, designed, and wrote, under various pseudonyms, eight issues of the fashion magazine *La Dernière Mode* (Fig. 6)—here, in this shop window tableau and in the glass's reflection, he experiences the crystallization of his linguistic delirium.

This poetic exploration of coincidence is what, later, André Breton was to cultivate and call "objective chance." It is what led him to the Paris flea market in search of the concrete materialization of his personal delirium around the phrase "Cinderella ashtray." What Breton found there was nothing more than a wooden salad spoon resting on a tiny lady's boot (Fig. 7).

Broodthaers's own tableaux carried the idea of the poetic object of Surrealism to another level. Starting with the plaster tomb he created for his final book of poetry, it continued to a kind of hilarious apotheosis in the idea of the installation and the private museum (here, he was especially prescient) of words, images, and things. These were often presided over by palms, symbols of victory (a reference to Belgium's colonialist past), and the ultimate imperial image of triumph, the eagle (Fig. 8).

Broodthaers had a poetic sensibility—he was, after all, a poet and did not stop being one after he became an artist. Perhaps it's true that, for Broodthaers, Mallarmé's masterpiece *Un Coup de Dés* was something like the zero-point of modernism. Mallarmé introduced into poetry the idea of a spatial distribution—something made clear by Broodthaers's own recasting of the entirely redacted poem as a cascade of black Malevich-style rectangles. After all, when exhibiting his version of the piece, Broodthaers saw fit to include an image of the author of *Un Coup de Dés* with the designation "Fig. 0" (Fig. 9).

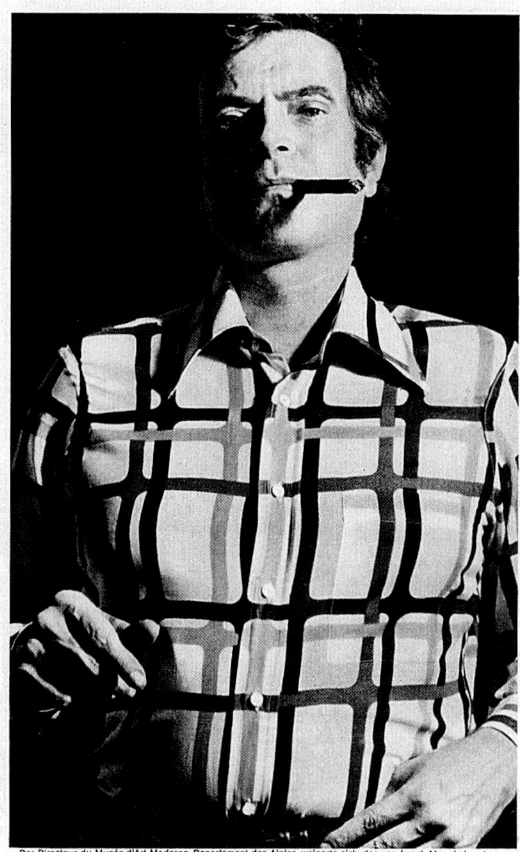

Fig. 1
Marcel Broodthaers, "Der Directeur du Musée d'Art Moderne, Département des Aigles, weigerte sich, das van Laack Monokel zu tragen" [The Director of the Musée d'Art Moderne, Département des Aigles, refused to wear the van Laack monocle]. Advertisement published in *Der Spiegel* No. 13 (March 22, 1971), 166. © 2016 Estate of Marcel Broodthaers / Artists Rights Society (ARS), New York / SABAM, Brussels

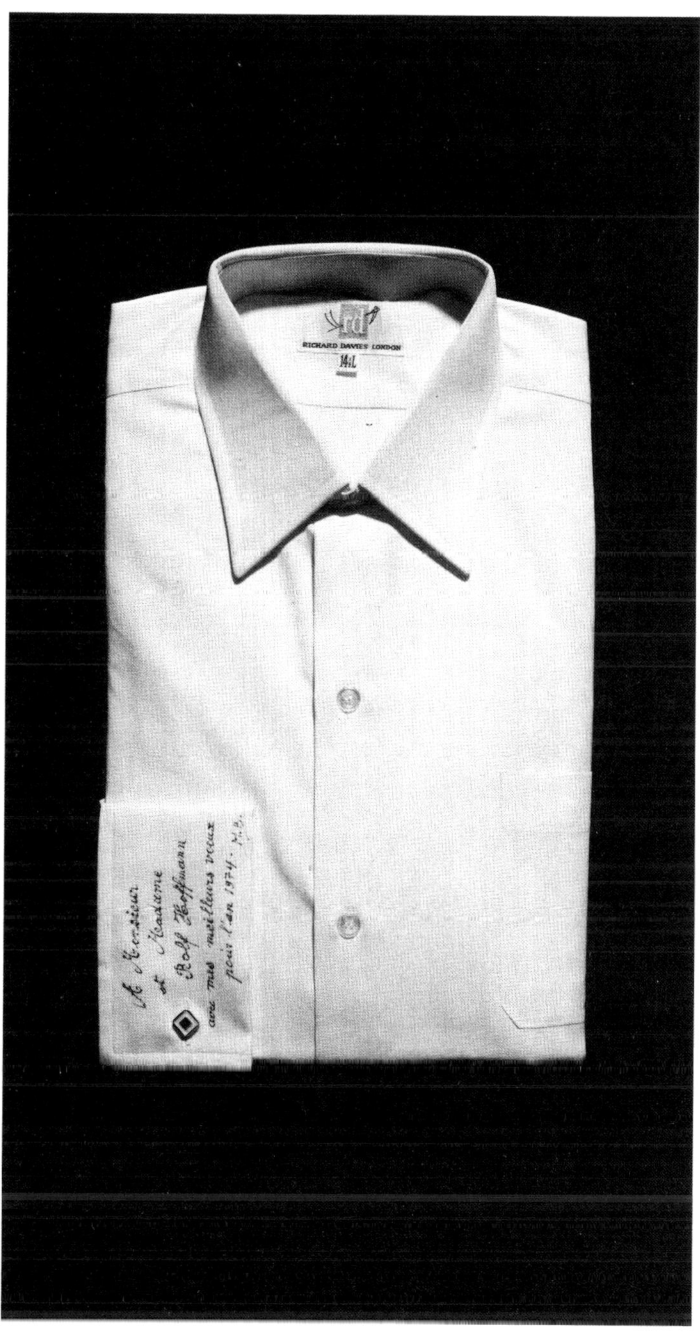

Kat. Nr. 106: A Monsieur et Madame Hoffmann . . ., 1974

Fig. 2
Folded white van Laack shirt given to the owners of the van
Laack company with a dedication from Broodthaers on the cuff

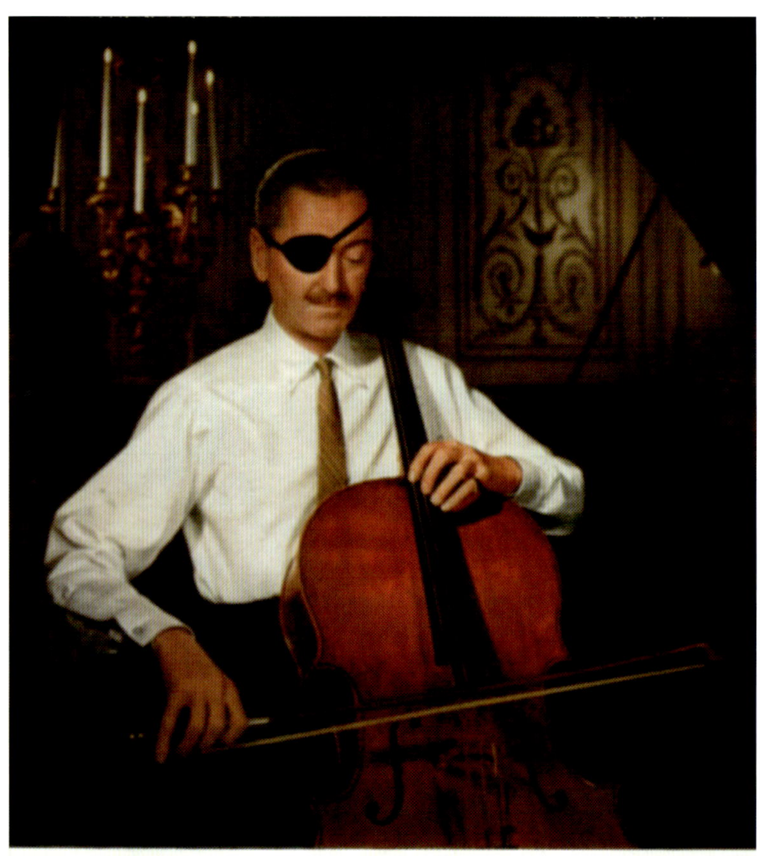

Fig. 3
Advertisement for C.F. Hathaway, a small shirtmaker from Maine, featuring David Ogilvy's Hathaway man with eye patch

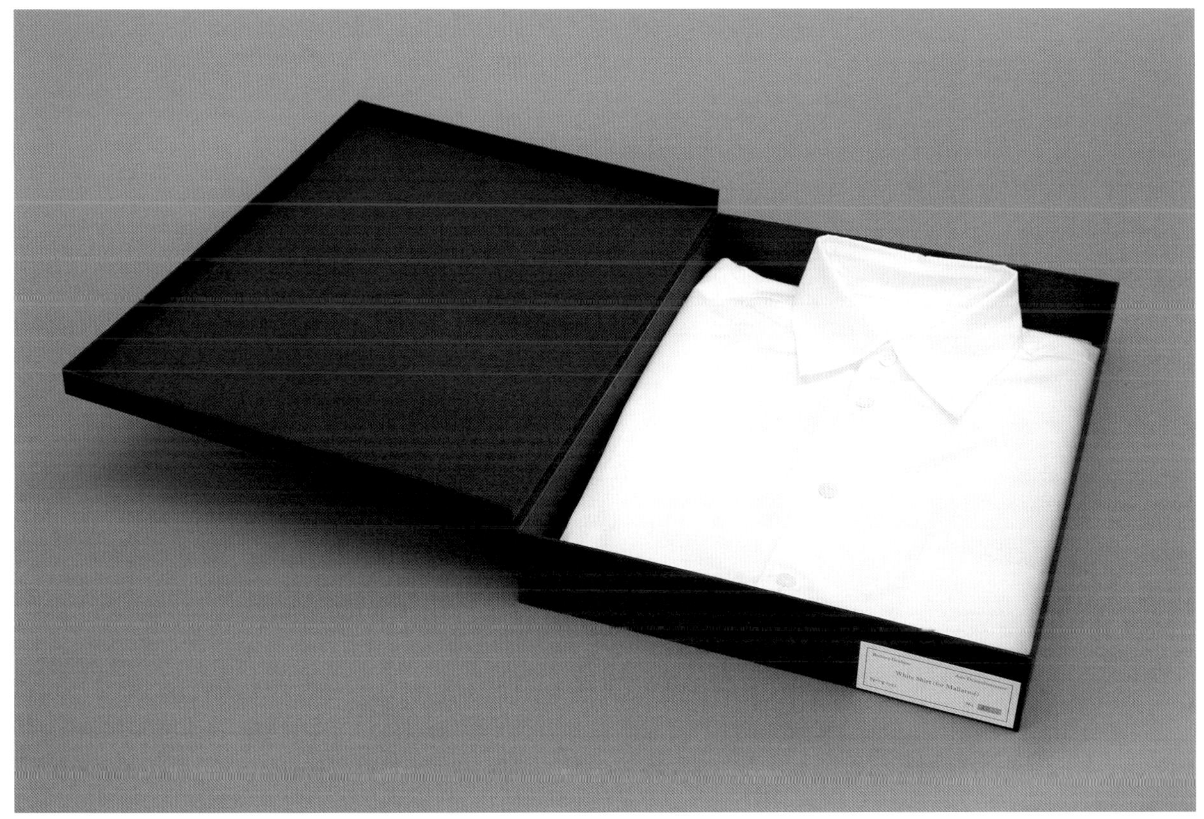

Fig 4
Rodney Graham, *White Shirt (for Mallarmé) Spring 1993*, 1992.
With the collaboration of Ann Demeulemeester. White cotton
shirt around handmade watercolor board and Japanese tissue
paper with Mallarmé poem in prose *The Demon of Analogy*,
16 1/3 x 12 3/5 x 2 1/3 in (41.5 x 32 x 6 cm). Courtesy the
artist. Photo: Scott Livingstone

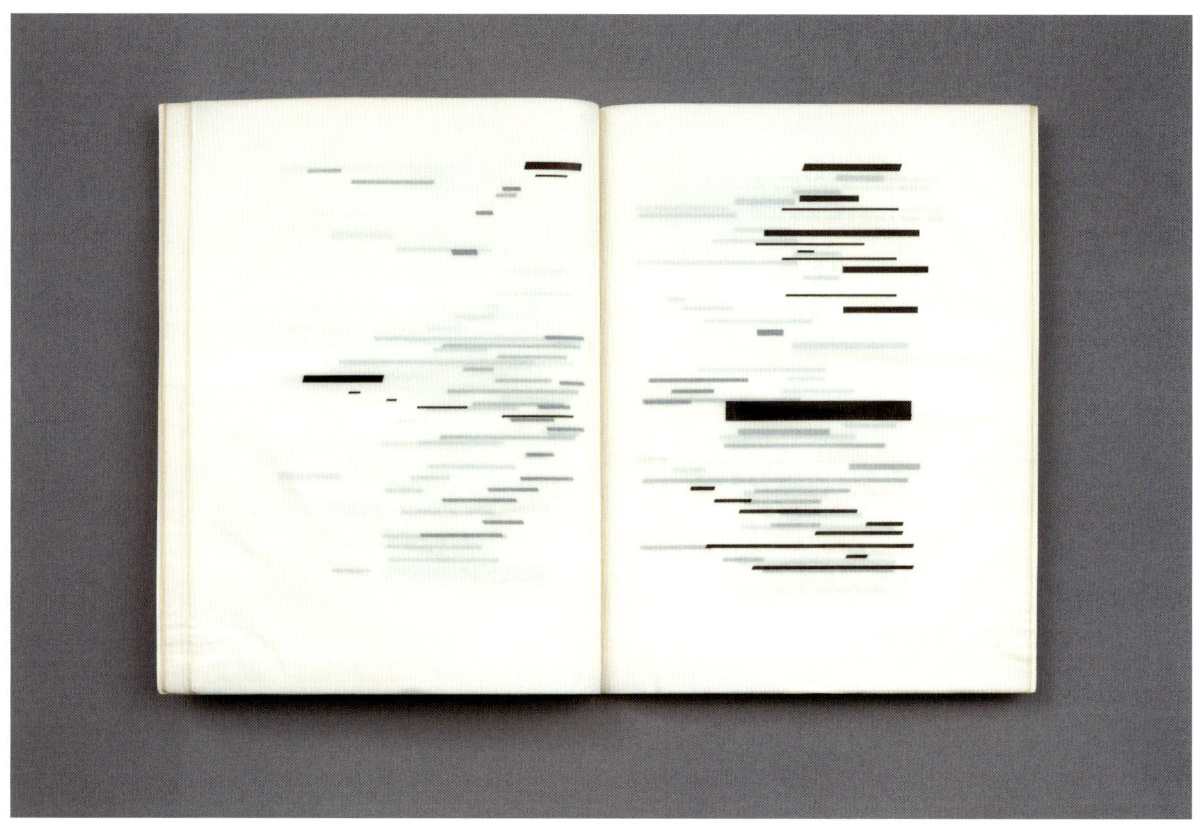

Fig. 5
Marcel Broodthaers, *Un Coup de Dés Jamais N'Abolira Le Hasard* by Stéphane Mallarmé, 1969. Twenty photolithographs, 12 3/4 x 9 13/16 in (32.4 x 24.9 cm). Museum of Modern Art; Purchased with funds given by Howard B. Johnson in honor of Riva Castleman. © 2016 Estate of Marcel Broodthaers / Artists Rights Society (ARS), New York / The Museum of Modern Art/ Licensed by SCALA / Art Resource, NY

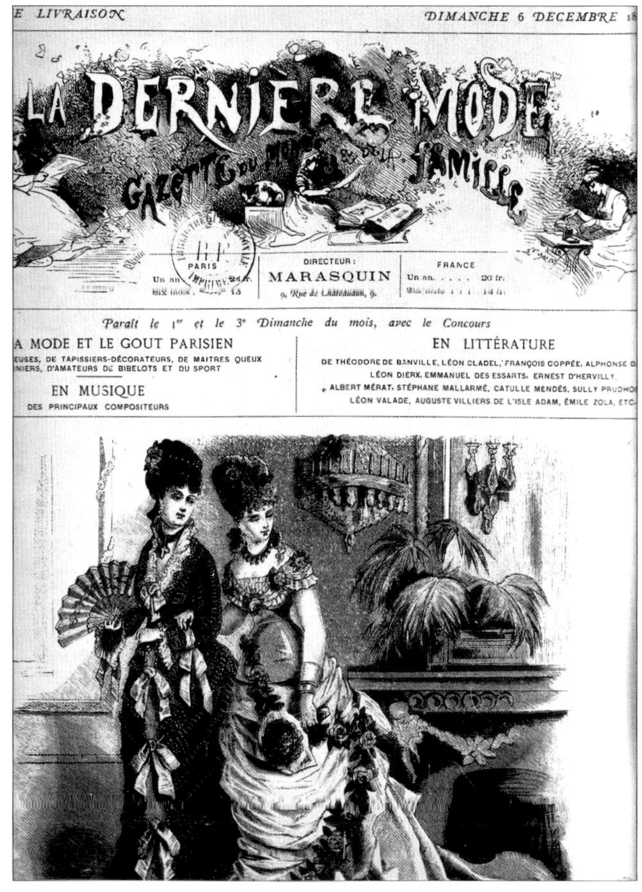

Fig. 6
Cover of the fashion magazine *La Dernière Mode*. Under
different pseudonyms Stéphane Mallarmé edited, designed,
and wrote eight issues of the publication

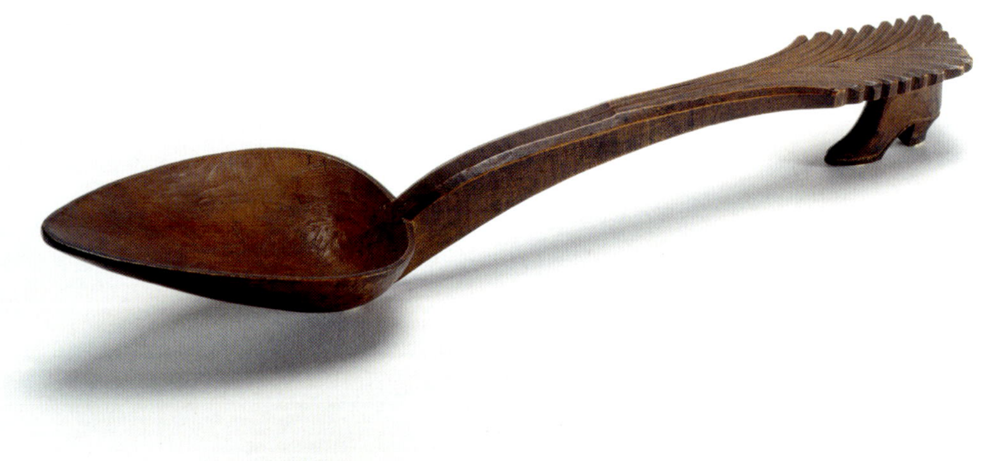

Fig. 7
Anonymous, *The big spoon. Large carved wood serving spoon*, owned by André Breton. Wood, 2 3/5 x 14 3/5 x 3 1/5 in (6.6 x 37.2 x 8.2 cm). Musée National d'Art Moderne, Centre Georges Pompidou, Paris. Photo: © CNAC/MNAM/Dist. RMN-Grand Palais / Jean-Claude Planchet / Art Resource, NY

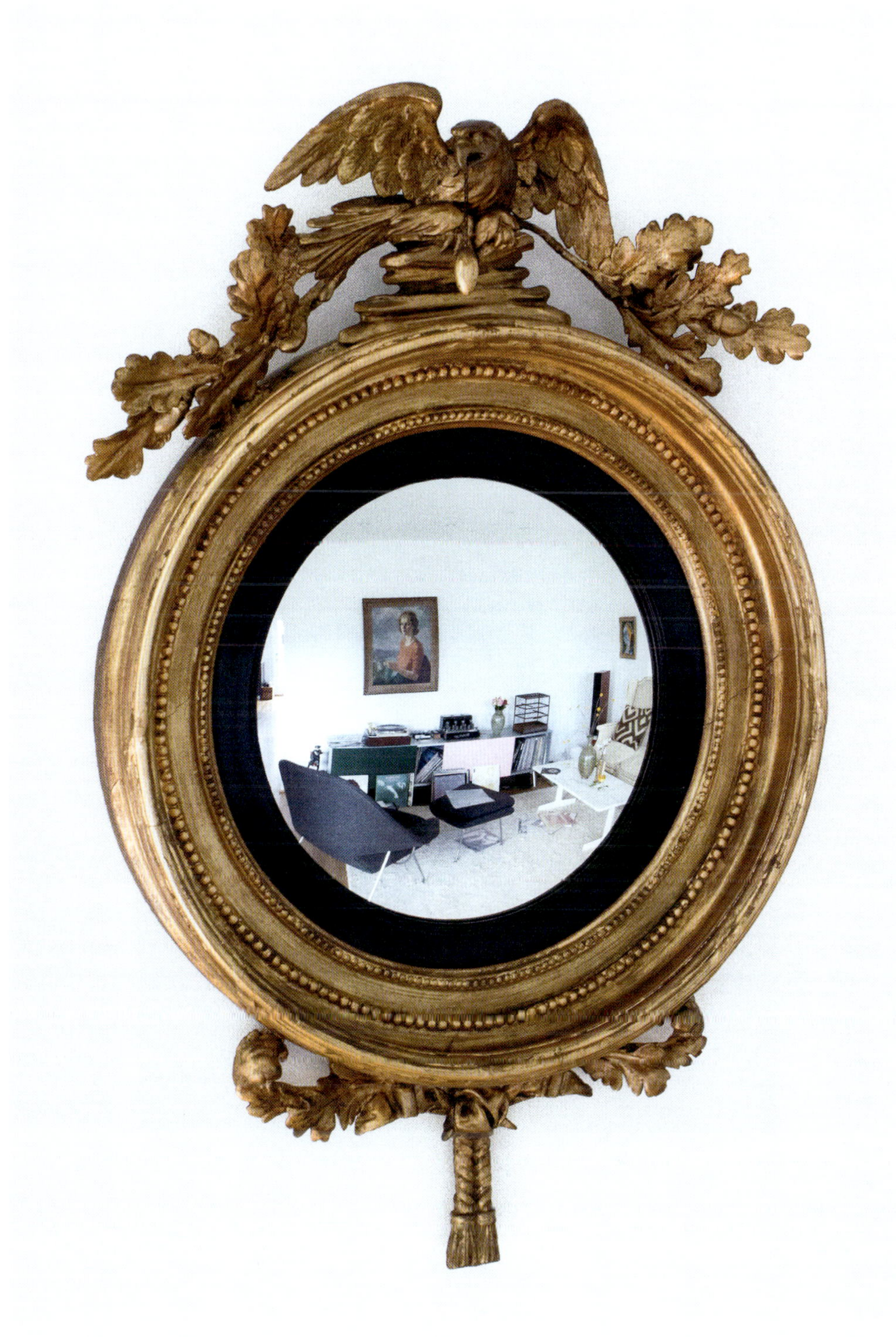

Fig. 8
The author's mirror. Photo: Scott Livingstone

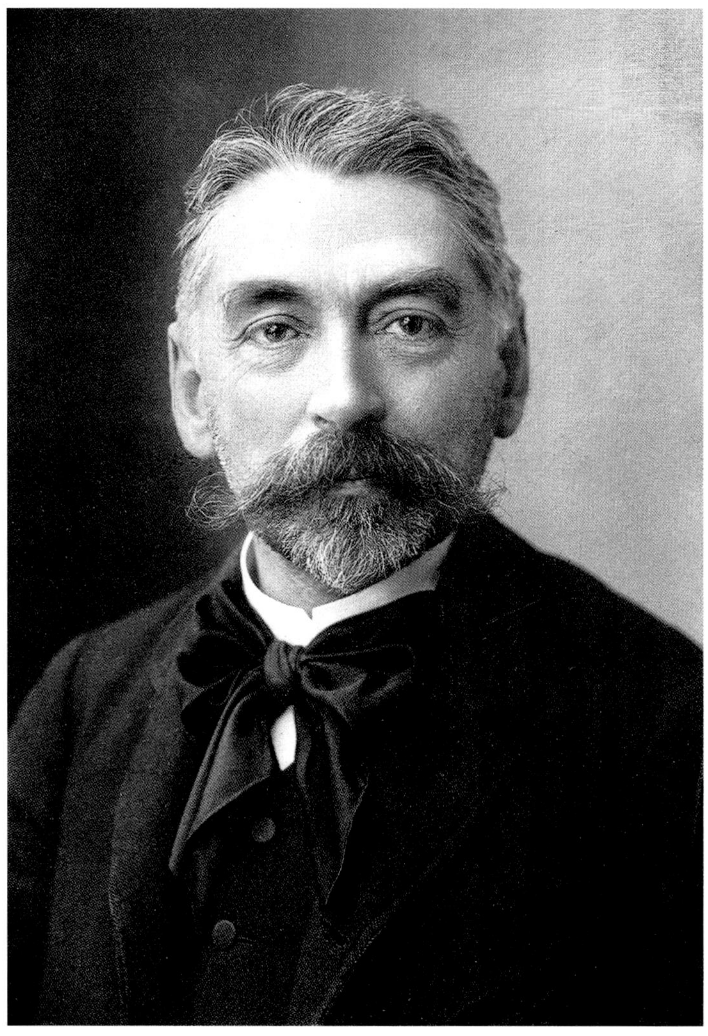

Fig. 9
Portrait of French poet and critic Stéphane Mallarmé (aka
Étienne Mallarmé). Born 1842, died 1898

Sarah Rifky
Keywords to Talking

This series of circumstantial reflections and narrations was originally drafted for a talk held at the Aspen Art Museum in April 2014. Since then, the political landscape in Egypt has been changing quite rapidly, and with it, the response of the civic and cultural community. The original draft has been edited; the sentiments and reflections from that time have been preserved, although the tense—in a temporal sense—has been updated to reflect the present. Accompanying this act of rewriting time, I am overseeing the closing of Beirut, *an art organization that was cofounded in Cairo in 2012 and is at the core of many reflections that compose this essay.*

Aspen

Last night, I learned that breathing—just breathing—is a
form of research. I was sleeping in my hotel room. I woke
up in a slight state of delirium, jetlagged, too warm,
and thirsty because of the room or the altitude. I had
just had a dream. In this dream, I had arrived in Aspen.
I was practicing regulating my breathing, for comfort,
but possibly also to prevent an anxiety attack. I saw a
laundry line. On it were hanging pairs and pairs of dark
socks. The socks were like paper bags, an aid for breathing.
They belonged to the people of Aspen. The sock attendant
informed me that by asking different people if I could
borrow their socks as breathing aids, I would improve my
capacity to breathe, and ultimately, I would learn more. I
woke up acutely aware that breathing—just breathing—is a
form of research.

Cleaning

We learn that with each individual moment of protest,
there is an acknowledgment of government, a bringing
into visibility some recognizable form. If one protests
a clause in a draft constitution, it affirms the prospect
of this constitution's becoming. Revolutions are about
housekeeping. You do a little bit every day; once a month,
you give the house a proper cleaning; and every six months
or so, you turn everything upside down. This might seem
like a banal comparison, but it is absolutely necessary. I
learned with time that sometimes we must resist being
activists for activism resists the position of doubt.
Doubt allows us to experience and not to overdetermine
things too quickly, bypassing imagination. I think the
most that can come from this way of describing things,
even if it marginalizes one intellectually, culturally, or
politically, is the possibility of reimagining a form of
politics that does not preside only over fixed affirmation.
Toward autonomy.

Observation

In the period between 2012 and now, a new wave of
institutions was founded in Cairo, in art and in culture.
Cultural workers linger in a haze of questions: What
is an institution? What can an institution be? How
do we organize? For self-organizing to occur, a self
needs to be identified. Many of these initiatives may
have existed already at an earlier point as desires, as
ideas. In those last few years, they have been finding
form as institutions. One peculiar observation is how
discipline arose to be desirable once again. Institutions
are becoming counter-dependent and discipline-bound.
You can see a very young institution forming solely for
art, another for cinema, a third for music, a fourth for
architecture, a fifth for journalism, and so on. It was
thought once that we would overcome boundaries and that
these limits of our subject would be asynchronous with
the present. I acknowledge that it is equally on the basis
of exclusion—and the negotiation between things—that
we render visible what we really seek to do, nurture, see
grow, and support.

Beirut

At first, there was a party. The best parties do not exclude great ideas. Some years ago, we were celebrating a friend's birthday at my place. We stood on the balcony peering at the villa beyond the trees. There stands a little house, a yellow villa, from the 1940s. It looks like a Belgian holiday home, which is odd considering that, at the time, we were in Cairo. A tad misplaced, but well nestled in the neighborhood of Agouza, this villa once housed the Middle East Studies Program (MESP), which had offered students a chance to learn Arabic and about the "modern Middle East" in a "Christ-centered manner." In 2011, following the uprising in Egypt, MESP decided to move. Cairo was not safe. MESP relocated to Jerusalem. The villa had stood empty for a year when, a few days after the party, Jens and I went to see it. Jens was visiting from Germany; we had met while we were studying in Malmö, Sweden. Later on he said, "It wasn't love at first sight"—he was speaking about the house. The space, quaint as it was, was a constant challenge to our imagination. Antonia joined us shortly after we started. And after some time, a love story ensued, but that's another tale. The three of us took on the task of imagining the institution every day. The institution itself was conceived on a whim, on a balcony during a party. *Beirut* was born. *Beirut* was an institution conceived on a whim for all the right reasons.

Time

The point of departure, the drive for us, was to become an ally of art at a time when art and artists were making way for other things—politically speaking. This moment then, three years ago, is different from this moment now, today. Thus, our mission was tweaked on a daily basis, and we wanted very much to test art as a site for thought without making the mistake of overthinking it; art that is sensitive and responsive, but not a "response" to things; art that acts, but that cannot be conflated with activism; art that is engaging, but not engaged, critical, and autonomous; art that is not propaganda; and most of all, art that is not entertainment. We wanted to do this for different reasons, some of which are our own. I wanted to do this for the city, for the community, and for ourselves. There was this moment of a fluid state, one continuously marked by political insurgency, a time of hope intertwined with crisis. And of course, you find yourself interpellated, your entire vocation thrown into sharp question: what is the role of art during these times?

Snowball

I've heard from curators I have a certain respect for that, for them, art functions symbolically. Perhaps they are right, but I am convinced that it does more. Art is an aggregator, but it can also aggravate. Art is one of the few spaces that allows for circumstantiality, association, and doubt. Art encrypts things. At *Beirut*, our concerns and questions were looking at not only artists and artworks, but also art institutions. What is the role of an art institution at a time of crisis? There was a moment when I stood in Aspen, by the river, beneath the mountains, and a simple thought drifted through my head. Crises are different wherever we go. Crisis doesn't have to be political necessarily, crisis can be emotional, environmental, in the kitchen, in the bedroom, in industry, education, parliament, congress...anywhere really. What is the role of art institutions vis-à-vis crisis? Do they have a response-ability toward crisis? The questions stop drifting, they are here to stay. Larger questions start forming into a snowball covered with desert sand. Before asking what the role of something is, perhaps we should also try to break down the question of what an institution is in the first place.

Statue

One beautiful way to think about the institution is to
behold it as a word. The word's Latin root, *statuere*, along
with the word "in" means "to establish" or "cause to stand."
It can mean stet, to let stand. It relates to status and
to statues.

Blessing

In the context of a collaboration with the Kadist Art Foundation, which enabled *Beirut* to host some thirty-five artworks on loan for a year, one of the artists involved, an established American woman artist, had mixed feelings about her participation. She expressed ambivalence to having her work be shown in Egypt, a country that was known for the mistreatment of women and had no respect for LGBTs, a country whose military regime had an awful human rights record and had become known for exercising military trials and executions. Then again, Egypt wasn't as notorious as other countries, she said, citing Uganda and Saudi Arabia. The artist reluctantly agreed to participate in the project with a "grudging ok" whilst stating: you don't have my blessings.

Her words lingered. The letter was hijacked from personal correspondence and recycled into my own notes. As persons, and as fictitious persons, as institutions, what is our role toward our governments? And from the perspective of the artwork, what rights does it have when it moves from the artist to another place, like a collection? Does an artist abstain from taking a strong political position because they feel that the decisions that underlie the movements of an artwork lie solely with those who "own" it? What does it mean to "own" an artwork? To not receive an artist's blessing for a work to be included in a show is a problem. Assent and blessings are important, just think of the traumas that connect all institutions from art to government to finance everywhere in the world.

Interview

In one of the interviews with a journalist, Jens replied to
his first question by stating, "*Beirut* does not exist." And
it's true. *Beirut* does not exist. For a time, *Beirut* existed
under the name of Goldin+Senneby Limited Liability
Company, but that's another artwork and another story
again. *Beirut* is a fiction, an invention, a name that, for
a certain amount of time, gave visibility to what we
do. We could never present what it is because it has
constantly been changing. Like institutions, countries,
and experience...*Beirut* changed, like how people change.
I came to think of *Beirut* not as an institution, but as
a means of role-playing an institution, a framework of
learning the institution by doing it.

Small

If you want something to stay small, start it big. This funny sentence makes a lot of sense. Although it wasn't intentional, it was something that we struggled with at *Beirut* for some time. Out of nothing, we had invented an institution. Like magic, through words, spells, actions, and quite a bit of work, we suddenly had a space with all the trimmings that make an art institution what it is. We had a curatorial seasonal structure, projects, visions, bank accounts—everything. We always argued that it was what Cairo needed at that moment and maybe we did too, to realize something, to externalize and see it. I often think about this small and big, and what size matters. I think of other stories of wisdom and I am sure I read something about the size of the mosquito compared to how powerful her sting can be. The mosquito demonstrates the art of timing, how she moves and progresses, when she rests and relaxes. In her own way, *Beirut* was a mosquito.

Water

I loved that for a long period of time, we were extremely articulate. We could easily and precisely identify what we did, and list our projects in an organized structure of seasons. *Beirut* comprised three seasons a year, and each season sprung from a set of interrelated questions. For example, our first season was looking at the relationship between labor and the image, grappling with what it means for the image to be a site of labor. We hosted the late filmmaker and dear friend Harun Farocki, who ran a workshop together with Antje Ehemann called Labour in a Single Shot; we held an exhibition of Maryam Jafri's work, *Global Slum*, which investigated sites that were constructed to be seen (like film locations) and thinking about the labor that takes place in them. We had four seasons that culminated in more than a year, moving between issues: from labor to institutions then to education. It worked, but also, it felt rushed. It felt too determined, like knowing without knowing, or performing something for an audience, and we thought, well that really can't be....

There is a question that comes up when reflecting on the brief history of *Beirut*, namely: how can an institution be like water? Like water so that it permeates things. Formless. How can an institution not force things, remain open and context-responsive. We asked ourselves frequently how *Beirut* could be open to constant revision and chance, reflecting a constant process of being reworked. Today, we also extend the very same questions to other art institutions, museums, collections, and biennials. Also, can the same questions be asked of institutions that are not art institutions? Can they become more fluid and more in tune with the natural order of things?

Balance

When you are trying to hold yourself together, can you balance your spirit and your body? When we started *Beirut*, we had every intention of being "mindful" of what we did, in not taking the institution for granted; at times, we found ourselves overtaken by the institution herself. It has been our task to learn to distinguish between what we did—the essence and core of what we were doing—and the body that was created, the fictitious person, the space and its demands, and what it served.

Thinking about institutions in practice demands a balance between two tiers of understanding, the conscious and the subconscious, the explicit and the implicit. How can we come to talk about the less apparent aspects of what we do? Our programs, our exhibitions, our productions had—and continue to have—circuits through which they are presented and shared to audiences and publics, in Cairo and elsewhere. What happens to the ruminations that want to take the art institution as a case study that is more than the sum of its parts? Artist Hito Steyerl in her essay *Politics of Art: Contemporary Art and the Transition to Post-Democracy* expands on curator Hongjohn Lin's notion that a standard way of relating politics to art assumes that art represents political issues in one way or another. Then again, there is a much more interesting perspective offered: the politics of the field of art as a place of work. Hito cogently adds: "Simply look at what it does—not what it shows."

Empty

There was one moment when, for several months, our art space stood empty. The emptiness was filled with a guilt that stemmed from years of being conditioned that doing is better than not doing, that action is better than not acting, and that knowledge is better than non-knowledge. Then I read Chapter 11 of the *Tao Te Ching,* the Chinese teachings of Tao, and something resonated:

> Mix clay to create a container
> In its emptiness, there is the function of a container
> Cut open doors and windows to create a room
> In its emptiness, there is the function of a room
> Therefore, that which exists is used to create benefit
> That which is empty is used to create functionality

We make a vessel out of mud, but it is the empty space that is useful to us. It is the intangible space, the void that is important...and this is the premise from which creating "spaces" can be understood as necessary. In Cairo, there is no path that is necessarily clear, literally or metaphorically. Yet, there is a unanimous unspoken realization and urge that has driven people to organize themselves into institutions and subsequently create spaces, even if they stand at times empty.

Hope

During the conference "The Times Are Changing: What will Art Do About it?" in Alexandria in 2012, the philosopher Franco Bifo-Berardi talked about the economics of decreasing wages and pension cuts. He also, as I remember, instructed the audience to "give up hope." It was something he had seen on a banner in Bucharest, and naturally, to have hope nowadays is difficult. It felt as though he had absolved us of the weight of expectation. We talked about the common ground, the shared experience, the shared sensibility between what has been happening in Europe and what has been happening south of the Mediterranean, North Africa, but also in cities across the ocean. This was some time before the exasperated issue of the Greek crisis. We all suffer from the predatory financial capital. There is no territoriality to the present ruling class, it's not just the disposing of a leader, a figure, a head of state, military-meddled state. What we are confronted with is abstract. The process of the accumulation of things is meaningless except for things that refuse to be accumulated. This poses a question in relation to art at a time of insurrection, particularly one followed by autocratic dictatorship: what types of traces, gestures, acts, and works refuse to be accumulated? To understand that, and to understand what is happening next, a more resolute concern with markets and economy, also in art, needs to be made manifest.

Account

We organize, we institute, we become accountable to one another, we are able to create a place from which to respond to one another, to assume positions, and to assume responsibility. Everyone is an owner, everyone is an entrepreneur, everyone is an artist. This relinquishing of one, this being an artist, a curator, an author, and becoming "it" (short for institution), performing an apparatus (like a collection of notes, not like capitalism)—even if fictitiously conceived—allows us to take care of each other and ourselves. A network of interdependent nodes or people in small groups: there is no union, syndicate, category, or class.

"Relax, give up hope," Bifo says. Stop thinking that the problem is about governing society, about institutions. We have to assertively create, produce, and invent a new totality in the face of capitalism. The political unconscious is based on replacing totalities. To give up hope is also to start thinking of the proliferation of autonomous forms of life and happiness. In art, to use signs that do not represent reality necessarily is key, conscious reality perhaps. Following through a desire of re-activating language outside of the place of financial language, and its dictatorship, to bring back the erotic, the sensuous understanding of the world, and to life in general. Bifo is romantic, and in some manner, also right.